THE BATTLE OF KORSUN-CHERKASSY

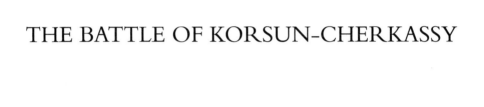

THE BATTLE OF KORSUN-CHERKASSY

The Encirclement and Breakout of
Army Group South, 1944

NIKOLAUS VON VORMANN

Translated by
GEOFFREY BROOKS

Series editor:
MATTHIAS STROHN

CASEMATE
Philadelphia & Oxford

AN AUSA BOOK

Association of the United States Army
2425 Wilson Boulevard, Arlington, Virginia, 22201, USA

Published in the United States of America and Great Britain in 2018 by
CASEMATE PUBLISHERS
1950 Lawrence Road, Havertown, PA 19083, USA
and
The Old Music Hall, 106–108 Cowley Road, Oxford OX4 1JE, UK

© 2018 Association of the U.S. Army

Originally published as Die Wehrmacht im Kampf 3: N. von Vormann, *Tscherkassy* (Kurt
Vowinckel Verlag Heidelberg, 1954)

Translator: Geoffrey Brooks
Series Editor: Matthias Strohn

Hardback Edition: ISBN 978-1-61200-603-1
Digital Edition: ISBN 978-1-61200-604-8

Cataloging-in-publication data is available from the Library of Congress and the British Library.

Printed and bound in the United States of America

For a complete list of Casemate titles, please contact:

CASEMATE PUBLISHERS (US)
Telephone (610) 853-9131
Fax (610) 853-9146
Email: casemate@casematepublishers.com
www.casematepublishers.com

CASEMATE PUBLISHERS (UK)
Telephone (01865) 241249
Email: casemate-uk@casematepublishers.co.uk
www.casematepublishers.co.uk

Cover image: Panzers and half-tracks, February 1944. (Bundesarchiv, Bild 101I-090-3913-24)

Contents

Foreword

Cherkassy. Who, except military history experts and those with a deep interest in World War II would associate this name of a city in modern-day Ukraine with a bloody battle that raged in January and February 1944? It is doubtful whether many people could point at Cherkassy on a map of modern-day Ukraine. And yet, this battle – often known in English as the battle of the Korsun-Cherkassy pocket after the smaller settlement Korsun approximately 70 kilometres to the west of Cherkassy – resulted in approximately 55,000 dead plus a much higher number of wounded soldiers. In a war of the early 21st century, this would make this battle stand out. In the context of the Eastern Front of World War II, this figure was, sadly, just another number added to the Reaper's long list of casualties between 1941 and 1945. And yet, this battle was special. Approximately 60,000 German soldiers, including some SS units, were encircled by the Soviets and in a desperate struggle these soldiers managed to break through the Soviet lines and were able to link up with the German relief forces. Both the Germans and the Soviets claimed the battle as their victory.

The man who wrote the German account of the battle that you now hold in your hands in the English translation was General der Panzertruppe Nikolaus von Vormann, one of the protagonists of the battle on the German side. He was born on 24 December 1895. He joined the Prussian Army as a young volunteer in August 1914 and in World War I he fought bravely and was highly decorated. After the war, he briefly served in a para-military Freikorps and then joined the Reichswehr, the 100,000-men army of the Weimar Republic. From then until the outbreak of the war, staff posts and unit command alternated, as was the German tradition for general staff officers. During World War II, he served predominately on the Eastern Front. In December 1942, he commanded 23rd Panzer Division, which was involved in Operation *Winter Storm*, the failed attempt to relief Sixth Army from the pocket in Stalingrad. In December 1943 he became the commander of XXXXVII Panzer Corps which under his command fought at Cherkassy and which was part of the relief force designated to reach the troops in the pocket or cauldron (*Kessel*) as the Germans referred to it. Later in 1944, after his promotion to *General der Panzertruppe*, he was given command of Ninth Army, which had suffered badly during the Soviet summer offensive. He ended the war as commandant of the 'Alps Fortress', to which he had been appointed on 4 May 1945. He died on 26 October 1959.

His career was a very successful example of the career of a professional officer in the Prussian/German Army. He was an effective unit commander and a diligent staff officer. This book is in many ways the result of Vormann's training and education. It describes the events of the battle with the quiet, detached style of the general staff officer, who keeps a calm head and is not panicked by the reports from the front line. The result is a portrayal of the battle that could be described as analytical and perhaps somewhat cold. This is particularly obvious in his description of the German break out from the pocket in chapter 8. The German attack did not go according to plan and was badly synchronised. As a consequence., the Soviets were able to cause horrendous casualties among the German troops who were desperately trying to escape the deadly encirclement of the pocket. The scene at hill 239, the point of main effort of the German break out, was pure carnage: during the night of 16/17 February, thousands of desperate German soldiers charged up the hill with fixed bayonets and were engaged by Soviet artillery, machine guns and tanks. It was sheer horror. Within minutes, the corpses of dead German soldiers covered the ground. This *danse macabre* reached its climax when the 5th Soviet Guards Cavalry Corps charged into the desperate German soldiers, riding down the exhausted enemy and killing them with their sabres. That night, approximately 20,000 German soldiers perished. Vormann only hints at this when he says that two German army corps had ceased to exist.

Vormann asks who was responsible for this senseless slaughter. He finds the answer very quickly and without too much searching: for him, the culprit was Hitler, who constantly interfered in the operational conduct of war on the Eastern Front. It is therefore not astonishing that quite a great deal of the book deals with Hitler, his responsibility for the defeat and the relationship between the soldiers and the population on the one side and Hitler on the other. Vormann wrote his book in 1954 and his general argument is one that can be found in many of the books published by former German generals in that period. The reason for this is clear: by putting the sole blame on Hitler, the German officer corps, in particular the General Staff, could be white-washed of any potential criticism of their conduct of operations. Today, we know that, as always, the reality was not black and white and that the role of the officer corps has to be seen in a different light. Naturally, Vormann, as a member of the German General Staff, was biased. Also, sources that are available now were not available in 1954, at the time of Vormann's writing. Therefore, it is important to read Vormann's words about Hitler and the operational excursions with a pinch of salt and one has to understand the context that shaped his book. This does not take away the fact that his account provides a very good account of the military issues and problems that surrounded the battle of the Korsun-Cherkassy pocket and it provides an insight into the mind of a German officer who played a very important role in this battle of 1944, which, unfortunately, was only one of the many battles of the maelstrom of the Eastern Front.

Dr Matthias Strohn, M.St., FRHistS.
Head Historical Analysis,
Centre for Historical Analysis and Conflict Research Camberley
Senior Lecturer, Royal Military Academy Sandhurst
Reader in Modern War Studies, University of Buckingham

Introduction

Frederick the Great was the last to have it in his power to be his own Chancellor and Supreme Warlord.

Napoleon tried but was unable to solve the problem.

Hitler made the attempt. He also failed; was weighed and found wanting.

Hitler became Chancellor through the guilt and failure of the political parties. In addition the Reichstag granted him voluntarily full dictatorial powers.

He crowned himself Supreme Warlord. He believed in his Mission. Something intangible which he called Intuition generated his operational orders. The advice of soldiers was not wanted. A unique situation in the history of warfare developed in full view: in the midst of war the soldier had no say. The politician even led the military operations as dictator.

After 1945 the generals were reproached for not having set themselves up as judges over the leaders of the land created by the politicians. Accordingly they suffered hanging, were thrown into prison, starved to death or went to wreck and ruin.

In 1918 the blame had fallen on Junkerdom and the clerics. In 1945 there was unity that the generals were responsible. And it was precisely those parties which had called Hitler forward and approved the 1933 Enabling Act which shouted the loudest: Stop thief! They forgot that it was they themselves who until then had stoned any soldier daring to voice a word of criticism or a political opinion. That was the case in the Weimar Republic until 1933 and much worse subsequently.

Now they were happy to have found, sitting defenceless and without means behind barbed wire, the whipping boys for their own failure.

Clausewitz' doctrine 'that war is only a continuation of political policy by other means, therefore has no independent nature' and that the politicians alone bear the responsibility for it 'for politics give rise to war' was disavowed.

This attempt to shift the blame after the collapse inevitably bore its fruit. It is important to be clear about the consequences. There is no longer, and will never be again, the unpolitical soldier who, following old tradition, carries out the instructions of the statesman as an organ of service.

If Chancellor and Supreme Warlord are no longer to be combined in one person, their respective jurisdictions must be clearly separated and defined. The enormous sum of wrong decisions by politicians after Bismarck compels the introduction of a control device which provides the soldier with the possibility of protecting himself against too much being required of him.

The prerogatives and obligations were hitherto distributed too unequally. Twice the politicians made the whole world our enemies under arms. In general their heads did not roll for their guilt or failure.

It was always the soldier at the front who had to foot the bill for what he had not created – and die, as at Cherkassy in the Ukraine in 1944.

von Vormann
Berchtesgaden 1953

Maps

Maps 2–10 portray the course of a great battle pictorially. They are not the products of postwar fantasy, but were made in 1944 during the fighting itself.

In order to present graphically the situation at the time, the groupings of both sides are shown simultaneously.

Knowledge as to the enemy's groupings and his intentions, as the maps show, are naturally known best at the end of a phase of battle of one or several days and not at the beginning. Our own movements were taken without this foreknowledge.

1. Army Group South: Sixth, Eighth, First Panzer, Fourth Panzer Army. Mid-January 1944.

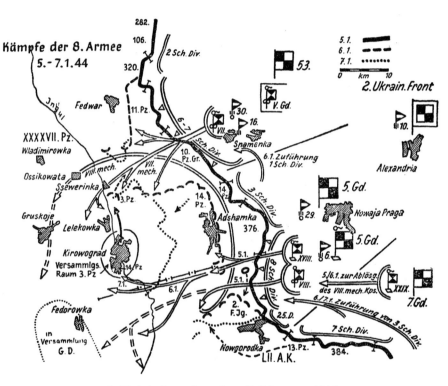

2. Eighth Army in action, 5–7 January 1944

3. Eighth Army in action, 8–10 January 1944

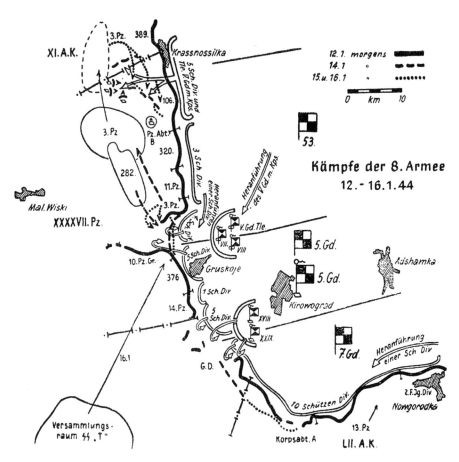

4. Eighth Army in action 12–16 January 1944

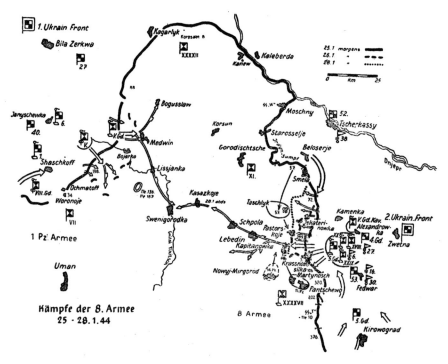

5. Eighth Army in action 25–28 January 1944

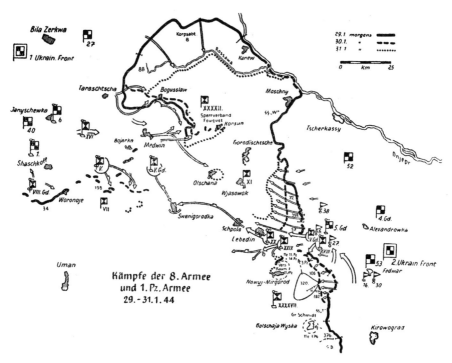

6. Eighth Army and First Panzer Army in action, 29–31 January 1944

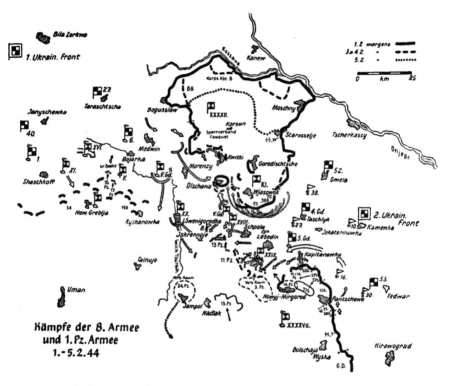

7. Eighth Army and First Panzer Army in action, 1–5 February 1944

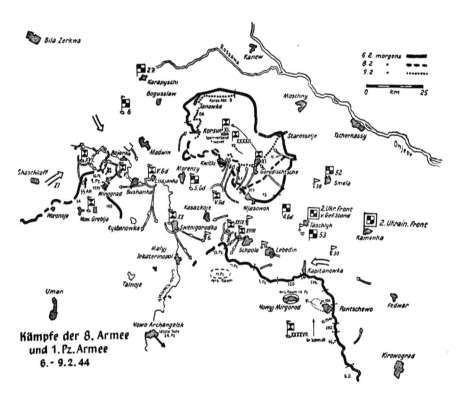

8. Eighth Army and First Panzer Army in action, 6–9 February 1944

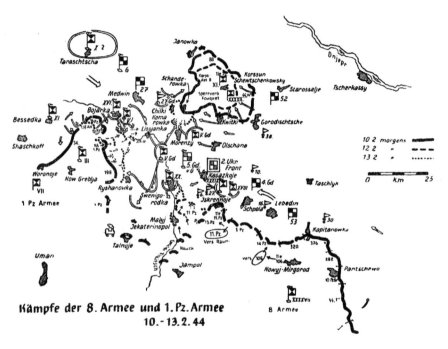

9. Eighth Army and First Panzer Army in action, 10–13 February 1944

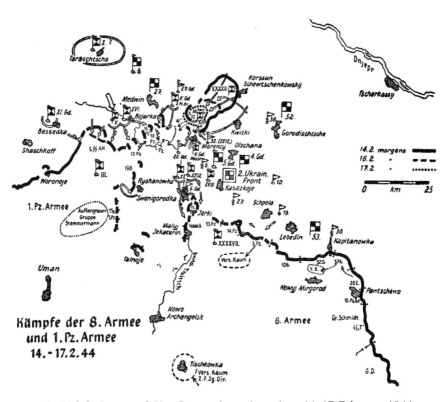

10. Eighth Army and First Panzer Army in action, 14–17 February 1944

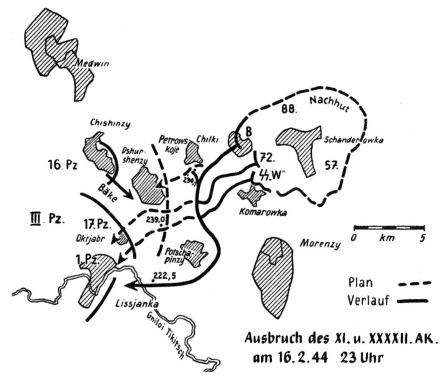

Medwin

Chishinzy

Petrows-
koje Chilki   B

Dshur-
shenzy   72.
16. Pz   ₄,W"   57.
          Bäke
                  234,7

III. Pz.   17. Pz.   Komarowka
          Oktjabr   239,0

1. Pz.   Potscha-   Morenzy   0   km   5
             pinzy
                    222,5

Lissjanka   Plan   - - -
Gniloi Tikitsch   Verlauf ———

88. Nachhut

Schanderowka

**Ausbruch des XI. u. XXXXII. AK.
am 16.2.44 23 Uhr**

11. Breakout of XI and XXXXII Army Corps at 2300 hrs on 16 February 1944

Place names:

German	English usage
Adshamka	Adshamka
Angerburg	Angerburg
Apostolowa	Apostolev
Balkan	Balkans
Bertechsgaden	Berchtesgaden
Berditschew	Berditschev
Bielow	Bielov
Schwarzes Meer	Black Sea
Bolschaja Wyska	Bolshaya Vyska
Bojarka	Boyarka
Brest Litowsk	Brest Litovsk
Bug	Bug, River
Buschanka	Bushanka-Kissyanka
Bjelaja Zarkow	Byelaya Zarkov
Kaukasus	Caucasus
Tscherkassy	Cherkassy
Cherson	Cherson
Chilki	Chilki
Chirowka	Chirovka
Chischinzy	Chishinzy
Clausewitz	Clausewitz
Krakau	Cracow
Daschkukowka	Dashukovka
Dnjepr	Dnieper, River
Djnepropetrowsk	Dniepropetrovsk
Don	Don, River
Donetz	Donetz, River

German	English usage
Dshurshenzy	Dzhurshenzy
Galanin	Galanin
Gniloi Tikitsch	Gniloi Tikich, River
Gorodischtsche	Gorodishche
Gruskoje	Gruskoye
Ingul	Ingul, River
Ingulez	Ingulec, River
Irdyn-Sumpf	Irdyn Marshes
Iskrennoje	Iskrennoye
Kamenka	Kamenka
Kanew	Kanev
Kapitanowka	Kapitanovka
Charkow	Kharkov
Kiew	Kiev
Kirowograd	Kirovograd
Komarowka	Komarovka
Korosten	Korosten
Korsun	Korsun
Kowel	Kowel
Krassonssilka	Krassnossilka
Krementschug	Kremenchug
Krivoi Rog	Krivoi Rog
Kwitki	Kvitki
Lebedin	Lebedin
Lelekowka	Lelekovka
Lissjanka	Lissyanka
Mala Vyska	Mal-Viski
Mauerwald	Mauerwald
Medwin	Medvin

German	English usage
Mius	Mius, River
Morenzy	Morenzy
Mosyr	Mosyr
Nadlak	Nadlak
Nikopol	Nikopol
Now Greblja	Novaya Greblya
Nowgorodka	Novgorodka
Nowyj Mirgorod	Noviy Mirgorod
Nowo Ukrainka	Novo Ukrainka
Odessa	Odessa
Oktjabr	Oktyabr
Olschana	Olshana
Ossikowata	Ossikovata
Pantschewo	Panchevo
Pastorskoje	Pastorskoye
Perwomeisk	Pervomaisk
Progebischtsche	Pogrebishche
Potschapinzy	Potchapinzy
Pripjet	Pripet
Pruth	Pruth
Radomysl	Radomysl
Roshnatowka	Roshnatovka
Rostow	Rostov
Rotmistrow	Rotmistrov
Ryschanowka	Ryshanovka
Sarny	Sarny
Schandorowka	Shandorovka
Shaschkoff	Shashkov
Schewtschenkowsky	Shevchenkovskiy

German	English usage
Schpola	Shpola
Smela	Smela
Snamenka	Snamenka
Ssewerinka	Sseverinka
Starosselje	Staroselye
Swenigorodka	Svenigorodka
Tarnopol	Tarnopol
Tischkowka	Tichkovka
Uman	Uman
Werschina	Vershina
Winniza	Vinniza
Winograd	Vinograd
Wladimrowka	Vladimirovka
Wjasowok	Vyasovok
Jampol	Yampol
Jekaterinowka	Yekaterinovka
Jerki	Yerki
Saporoshje	Zaporozhye
Tschitomir	Zhitomir

German and British Ranks

German rank	British rank
Oberleutant	First Lieutenant
Major	Major
Oberstleutnant	Lieutenant-Colonel
Oberst	Colonel
Generalmajor	Major-General
Generalleutnant	Lieutenant-General
General	General
Generaloberst	Colonel-General
Generalfeldmarschall	Field Marshal

CHAPTER I

The East Wall at the Dnieper

The battle of Stalingrad came to a head at the beginning of 1943. It showed the world that the German Army was not invincible. The destruction of this myth was more painful than the loss of an entire army.

'This is the beginning of the end,' we felt instinctively at the front, and our heads told us that it was so, but not our hearts.

The Russians capturing Berlin was unimaginable. The mind refused to entertain this outcome. The One-Thousand-Year War against Asia could not end that way. That could not be the purpose of world history, not the outcome of unparalleled achievements. The front did not admit defeat – but it began to doubt.

Around the turn of the year 1942/43, under gruelling stress, the great retreat began at the southern end of the Russian Front. From the Volga and Caucasus the armies flooded back across the Don and Donetz towards the west. The Russians were quicker. By mid-February their tanks around Dniepropetrovsk barred the way over the Dnieper to the Reich.

Once again it proved possible to avert threatened disaster. From the midst of the retreat, Field Marshal von Manstein assembled his exhausted divisions for a series of attacks. The troops trusted his leadership. Everything that the Soviets had gained during their pursuit by outflanking so boldly over the Mius and central Donetz to the west was wiped out, even Kharkov was recaptured. A cohesive front was re-established behind the Mius and the central sector of the Donetz. With an effort it held together until September. Then finally it broke, and the retreat continued to the Dnieper.

Behind the Dnieper (Map 1)

In war, nothing is predictable. People run it, and people are not machines. Particularly in critical situations they can develop ideas that the commander has to consider and take into account if they have arisen without any action on his part. If he does not do that, or is unable to do it because he no longer has the pulse of the men, setbacks are inevitable. The mass thinks and acts differently to the individual. Panic, mutinies, even the laying down of arms can be the consequence, a chain of events that cannot be predicted by an outsider. This is a home truth from time immemorial – yet always forgotten. Mass psychoses and their consequences are known from every military campaign in history.

A mass psychosis of that nature occurred in the summer of 1943 on the southern front in the Soviet Union. The man in the front line dreamed of being safe behind the Dnieper. In all the heavy fighting of the previous months the only sensible thought he could hold onto was to get to the other side of the river and finally get some peace. This fixed idea, this dream, had enabled him to withstand the most horrific emotional burdens.

Never in the world history of war have troops spent almost a whole year fighting and retreating over hundreds of kilometres without the force eventually collapsing. The German Army of 1943 accomplished this unique achievement. The divisions from the southern front were probably groggy and exhausted but not broken.

They were capable of fighting and ready to fight; in their minds, this was the plan of the military leadership. They were obsessed by the concept of the strong East Wall behind the Dnieper with trenches behind barbed-wire entanglements, concrete bunkers, surveyed artillery emplacements and so on. There was no doubt in their minds that all this must be being built meanwhile and with all technological means available.

I was commanding 23rd Panzer Division and believed in it myself. I also wanted to sleep at night free from the fear that I would be awoken by Soviet tanks. The division had set out from Kharkov eastwards in the summer of 1942 and had fought in the Caucasus, outside Stalingrad, at the Manytsh river, at the Don, the Mius and the Donetz. On 25 September 1943, it was the last German panzer unit to pass through the burning factory district of Dniepropetrovsk and cross to the western bank of the river.

The disappointment of the troops was enormous, heart-rending to experience. There had been no preparations made for their arrival. The setting up of positions to the rear had been forbidden by Hitler expressly on the cynical basis that if they existed, his generals would always be looking to the rear. This resulted in a severe blow to the existing confidence in the highest level of leadership. Despair was unburdened in sarcastic ridicule when the regiments were given impossibly long sectors to defend. When the unit commanders had the opportunity to consult the map which showed the big picture – forbidden for them to see – they stood shaking their heads in disbelief.

The salient in the Dnieper bulged out as far east as Zaporozhye, from Kiev to the Melitopol bridgehead was 600 kilometres. By moving farther back to the Kiev–Nikolayev line following the Ingul river the front could be shortened by 200 kilometres, and if the Crimea were evacuated the entire Seventeenth Army relieved and made an operational reserve.

Hitler declined to consider such proposals for a number of reasons. After the defection of Italy he feared losing Hungary, Bulgaria, Rumania and also Turkey if the front edged any nearer the Balkans. He could also not relinquish the highly productive Ukrainian farms nor the manganese mines of Nikopol and Krivoi Rog. Finally, after the military setbacks on all fronts, he was concerned with the loss of prestige suffered in the eyes of the world.

Accordingly politics and economics held sway over military considerations and so the outcome was inevitable.

Under the strict order 'Hold at all costs', Army Group South was a chained dog at Zaporozhye, tasked with guarding the Dnieper as far north as Chernobyl north of Kiev, where it abutted the southern flank of Army Group Centre. The chain was too short. The north-east flank between Dniepropetrovsk and Kiev was over 400 kilometres long. The river was certainly an obstacle in places, but at best one could only speak of defences that stood behind it, never of a front.

The German forces located here were:

1. Sixth Army, Colonel-General Hollidt, either side of Melitopol
2. First Panzer Army, Colonel-General von Mackensen, later General Hube, either side of Dniepropetrovsk
3. Eighth Army, General Wöhler, from Kremenchug to Kanev
4. Fourth Panzer Army, Colonel-General Hoth, either side of Kiev
5. Manstein's HQ (Army Group South) was Hitler's former HQ *Wehrwolf* at Vinniza on the Bug river

The weakness of the German Dnieper defences cannot possibly have escaped the attention of the Soviets. The battlefield was their own country and their reconnaissance forays in the autumn of 1943 were as good as successful everywhere. Under the prevailing conditions their most promising plan was a major offensive with their combined forces to the south and south-west through Kiev or Cherkassy. This would have led unfailingly to an encirclement of the entirety of Army Group South between the Carpathians and the Black Sea. Based on their previous experience, this plan guaranteed additionally that Hitler would accept battle. Therefore all preconditions existed for success for the Soviets. After this great far-reaching leap all that remained was to tie off the neck of the bag and the War in the East would have ended at the latest by the beginning of 1944. Instead, the Soviet commanders dissipated their energies in minor operations along the whole front.

This was incomprehensible and we began searching for the motive for such peculiar behaviour. Unfortunately we had no reason to suspect that the cause could be the incompetence of the Soviet military leadership. Even an overestimation of the German forces, which might have daunted them in their decision, was not an acceptable explanation given the situation. Therefore the only conclusion to be inferred was that the Soviets, much depleted in men and materials, no longer felt able to conduct long-range operations. Even the official German version said so, and there was much to support it from what we ourselves had experienced.

Over preceding months it was not the quality of enemy troops but the quantity that had dominated the situation and brought them their successes. What had stormed our thin defensive lines was often enough not worthy of the terms 'soldiers' and 'troops'. They were mixed, untrained, poorly uniformed, poorly armed hordes. Like a spring tide they rolled in and flooded the area behind our lines if they met no resistance in the endless expanses of terrain. On the other hand, if they encountered an intact unit or were caught by panzers, their losses were horrific, exceeding all imagination.

The supply of people was inexhaustible, however; again and again the shining Soviet organisation would conjure up fresh hordes apparently from thin air. Close to the west bank of the Don battalions of women attacked our lines, its members only a few days previously having cooked for us and done our laundry at Rostov. At the Donetz a whole regiment infiltrated our lines by night without our infantry patrols noticing. At daybreak they were all rounded up: of the thousand men we captured, only one in twenty had a weapon and more than half were barefoot. One can supply any number of such examples.

If one puts forward foibles or weakness of character for the inexplicable behaviour of the highest Soviet leadership, then Hitler was right when he made no forces available to build the East Wall on the Dnieper, but his order subsequently to hold out there whatever the cost was cynical. Defence is passive sufferance. It cannot bring a decision, at best it gains time. We had no time to gain, for time was working against us. We had surrendered in North Africa, Italy had deserted us and invasion was threatened in France.

Clausewitz wrote: 'A swift, powerful transition to the attack – the flashing sword of retaliation – is the most brilliant point of defence. Whoever does not have it constantly in mind, or more so, whoever does not include it within the term defence, he will never understand the superiority of defence.'

We lacked this flashing sword of retaliation in our thinking. We didn't see the superiority of defence. Our morale was and remained low. We felt that we had lost the initiative and that from now on it was dictated by the enemy.

Defence

'It is a law: no battle is won from trenches, only from movement.'

This was taught by Alfred Graf von Schlieffen, from 1891 to 1906 Chief of the Kaiser's Grand General Staff. His successors did not like the doctrine and in August 1914, beset by anxieties, watered down the ingenious campaign plan against France. They thought they knew best. Passive defence gave the Soviets full freedom of manouevre and they used it.

The moving up and necessary regrouping of the Red Army was completed swiftly. The former army groups were renamed so that from now on the respective armies faced each other roughly in this order:

Sixth Army	4th Ukrainian Front, General Tolbuchin
First Panzer Army	3rd Ukrainian Front, General Malinovski
Eighth Army	2nd Ukrainian Front, General Koniev
Fourth Panzer Army	1st Ukrainian Front (southern flank), General Watutin
Fourth Panzer Army	1st White Russian Front (northern flank) and 2nd Army, Marshal Rokossovski

On 9 September 1943 the Soviet Army bulletin reported the resumption of their attacks along the entire front. These were pure containment operations, i.e. they created the basic requirements for future actions. They fulfilled their purpose. We allowed them to pin us down while we fought for the possession of territory.

It had become more important to hold some filthy village with an unpronounceable name in the back of beyond than to force our will on the enemy, the only objective for which a war is fought. Our thinking had become confused. It was the Soviets who determined the battlefield, the beginning and end of the individual battles. From being the hammer we had become instead the anvil.

In these weeks the same procedure was played out over and over again. Unopposed and undisturbed somewhere the enemy prepared his next attack. On our side the counter-measures had already been ordered from above: hold out at all costs, reserves are not available. The development then ran its programmed course: our defenders in that sector were overwhelmed, their losses in dead and wounded high, weapons and equipment lost.

Permission had to be wrested from the Führer to withdraw from the front individual units that at the moment seemed safe.

On the battlefield it might be that the enemy was on the point of breaking through. The freshly recruited reserves were rushed up and tossed hastily into the battle. The 'brilliant sword of retaliation' was regularly too blunt and too weak. Moreover, if we won limited local victories they were obtained at too high a price. They never brought a real decision, at best only slowing the development of catastrophe in the locality. When through the enemy's own losses the respective numbers present began to balance out, the Soviets would break off the attack leaving us to dig in exhausted where we happened to be. Generally after a few days the same game would be played at a different spot along the over-extended and under-defended front.

Thus, still in 1943, we lost Melitopol, Zaporozhye, Dniepropetrovsk, Kremenchug, Cherkassy and Kiev for a high price in blood. Before the year was out the front along the Dnieper ran from Cherson (near the Black Sea) to Nikopol – then inland to Krivoi Rog (Ingulec river) to Kirovograd (Ingul river) and from there back to the Dnieper above and below Cherkassy: then from Kanev (Dnieper) west to Byelaya Zarkov and from there north-west to Radomysl and Korosten. From here northwards to the southern flank of Army Group Centre at Mosyr in Pripet was a gap of 100 kilometres that we lacked the troops to close.

For all that, by Manstein's quality of leadership at least within Army Group South the connection was protected. It still did not appear to us that the war was lost militarily. Only the nature of leadership in battle in the south of the Eastern Front had to undergo a fundamental change. The possibility for it still existed.

The news leaked to us through secret channels regarding the conference of the Big Three in Teheran at the end of November, in which they agreed that the only terms on offer to Germany were unconditional surrender. This strengthened rather than weakened our will to fight on. The award of a Teutonic knight's sword by Churchill to Stalin to the strains of the Internationale (29.11.1943) was greeted with disgust. Vague hopes arose that the alliance of the unequal partners might be on the verge of collapse if a man such as Churchill were forced to participate in an unworthy theatrical of that kind.

An army corps in the East 1944 (Maps 1, 2, 5)

At the end of December 1943 at Berchtesgaden I received a telephone message to take immediate command of XXXXVII Panzer Corps. The well-known Führer Order that the military knowledge of any man should not extend beyond the limits of his own immediate area of jurisdiction was so strictly observed that I could not even find out at which end of Europe the corps was to be found. Full of expectations I proceeded to Army High Command (OKH) in the Mauerwald near Angerburg in East Prussia.

I stood before the huge situation map looking with incredulity at all the individual units on the Eastern Front up to division and battle group size. My enquiries as to the sense of a crooked front line like that was met with adverse criticism of myself or a resigned shrug of the shoulders: Führer's orders. The mood was unpleasant and despondent. Only the manner in which Zeitzler, Chief of the General Staff, outlined my new area of responsibility sounded confident but it seemed unnatural and forced. My efforts to learn something here at least about the future planning were unsuccessful. The last resort again: the position is to be held. I was not invited to present myself to Hitler.

I found XXXXVII Panzer Corps at Kirovograd, part of Eighth Army (command post, Novo Ukrainka). On the flight to the army group at Vinniza the pilot made a turn westwards over Brest Litovsk–Lemberg; such a large one that I asked him the reason for the deviation. 'It has always been risky over the Pripet marshes but now everything there is in movement. There's said to be some new dirty business in the offing from Kiev, and how far away the Russians are I have no idea. Safe is safe.'

Vinniza is on the Bug river just a little north of the important railway line Cracow–Lemberg–Tarnopol–Odessa, the last stretch of track still in German hands north of the Carpathians, the lifeline for all of Army Group South.

On 29 December the town had a familiar unpleasant look about it: from north to south streamed columns and rear echelons of Fourth Panzer Army, communications detachments and party service offices. The army group was also on the point of heading for Lemberg.

On Christmas Day, 1st Ukrainian Front under General Watutin had resumed its advance from Kiev and had already reached Berditschev–Zhitomir–Korosten. North of there through the gap between Army Groups Centre and South the Soviet masses flooded unchecked south of the Pripet marshes to the west towards Sarny. The pressure was increasing continuously to the south and south-east.

Thus what seemed to be afoot was what had long been indicated by the maps and movements of forces: the encirclement of all Army Group South between the Carpathians and the Black Sea. In any case, when I set out on the journey to Eighth Army I had the feeling that a gate was about to slam shut behind me.

More than 400 kilometres east of Vinniza is Kirovograd, almost in the farthest corner of the deep pocket. Hitler had placed the strictest embargo on any evacuation, pointing to the successes – as opposed to the alternatives recommended by the Army General Staff – which had resulted from his orders to give no ground in the crisis winter of 1941. Colonel-General Jodl wrote from his prison cell after the war's end: 'I never admired Hitler more than the winter of 1941, when he alone brought the tottering Eastern Front to a standstill, when his will and determination penetrated to the most advanced lines, exactly as in the last war when Hindenburg and Ludendorff took over the OHL (Supreme Army Command). Any other representation is a falsehood which slaps historical truth in the face.'

Then as now the front thought otherwise. The winter of 1941 broke the spine of the Army and undermined the feeling of superiority over the Red Army. Stalingrad and the retreats of 1943 had struck a heavy blow to our confidence in Hitler and also – regrettably – in our own capabilities while the autumn fighting on the Dnieper had almost consumed the last of our strength. The troops, asked again and again to do more than the possible, had not been crisis-proof for a long time and were very sensitive to any threat on the flanks. The spectre of encirclement haunted them and was fed by the madness of the 'strongpoints'.

Therefore my expectations were by no means optimistic when I assumed command of XXXXVII Panzer Corps on New Year's Eve 1943. It was located east and north-east of Kirovograd with 376th Infantry Division (Major-General Schwarz), 14th Panzer Division (Major-General Unrein), 10th Panzer-Grenadier Division (Lieutenant-General Schmidt), 11th Panzer Division (Lieutenant-General von Wietersheim), 320th Infantry Division (Lieutenant-General Postel), 106th Infantry Division (Lieutenant-General Forst) and 282nd Infantry Division (Lieutenant-General Frenking). After a few days the formation was joined by 3rd Panzer Division (Lieutenant-General Bayerlein). Apart from a few 11th and 14th Panzer Division panzers no reserves were available.

Northwards to the Dnieper were XI Army Corps (General of Artillery Stemmermann) with 389th, 72nd, and 57th Infantry Divisions and 5th SS-Panzer Division *Wiking*.

Bent back from the Dnieper to east of Shashkov was the area held by XXXXII Army Corps (Lieutenant-General Lieb) with Corps Abteilung B, 88th and 198th Infantry Divisions (until 28 January under First Panzer Army).

From 5 January, LII Army Corps with 2nd Parachute Division, 13th Panzer Division and 384th Infantry Division south-east of Kirovograd came under the command of Eighth Army.

None of the divisions could be described as even close to operational strength. According to their numbers the panzer divisions were at best armoured groups, the infantry divisions reinforced regiments in the old sense. Some of them were so short of horses that it limited their capability to move. The condition of the individual battalions and smaller units was alarming. The bitter cold, enemy action and lack of equipment further restricted their limited fighting strength. Because the corps had to defend a front line of about 100 kilometres in length, the sectors allotted to the individual units were so long as to defy all reason.

Far behind us to the west in the first days of January 1944 the front seemed to waver continually. The Soviet thrust through the gap between Army Groups South and Centre, which would very soon cross the old Polish border at Luzk and Kovel, was covered by means of powerful attacks of their 38th and 40th Armies to the south across the line

Byelaya Zerkov–Berditschev. The 1st Ukrainian Front came up against no resistance worth mentioning there. The weak German units flowed back towards Bug river. Vinniza was enveloped, the route to Uman, west of Kirovograd, as good as clear. General Hube, First Panzer Army, who until then had commanded in the so-called 'pocket' around Apostolov, was selected to stop the rot by a counter-attack. He was given a few divisions much too weak for the task so that from the outset no penetrating success could be expected. Our lifeline, the railway connection between Lemberg and Odessa, remained under threat.

Sixth Army took command of the area between Cherson on the Black Sea coast to south of Kirovograd. The Army Group South front line now no longer faced east, but roughly north over the 1,000 kilometres between Nikopol and Kowel on the Polish border.

CHAPTER 2

The battle of Kirovograd

Strategic plans (Maps 1, 2)

This was the situation at the beginning of January when ground-, radio- and air reconnaissance predicted new Soviet preparations to attack Eighth Army dispositions on the Eastern Front. The 2nd Ukrainian Front under General Koniev had moved up.

It had been established that the 5th Soviet Guards Army was astride the boundary with Sixth Army south of Kirovograd; 53rd Soviet Army, with 5th Soviet Guards Tank Army to the rear, north of Kirovograd.

The very open and irresponsible lively Soviet radio traffic left no doubt that the launch of the offensive was imminent.

The enemy's intentions could be read from the map. If General Koniev's 2nd Ukrainian Front gained territory to the west via Kirovograd, it would very soon link up with 1st Ukrainian Front under General Watutin, which was already making good headway across the Vinniza–Uman line towards the Bug river. From Kirovograd to Uman as the crow flies is only 150 kilometres. If the two Soviet army groups met up in the Uman–Pervomaisk area (only 100 kilometres from Kirovograd), the War in the East was as good as over, for it would lead in quick succession to the elimination of Eighth Army, the encirclement of Sixth Army, Seventeenth Army in Crimea and the rolling-up of First and Fourth Panzer Armies fighting with no support to their right or left.

The Soviets had used the time which our inactivity allowed. The attacks aimed in previous months at pinning us down had achieved their aim: we had remained in the pocket at the lower Dnieper. The epoch of pinning us down was past. Stalin was ready, had rested his troops and was now going for the kill. Once again it had been left up to him to choose the where and when of battle.

The German supreme commander still had freedom to manouevre, to accept or decline the offer of battle. The hour for making major new operational decisions had come and gone. In the East we had long been inferior in numbers regarding personnel and materials, but superior in quality. Our military commanders and troops were better than those of the Soviets. The chance existed with mobile warfare to annihilate the Red hordes through swift, flexible operations. What was needed was courage to break free of the deceptive security of the trenches. The OKW could not make this decision. We received our customary orders to battle on and hold our ground 'at all costs'.

The task which Hitler gave Eighth Army seemed almost impossible. He persisted in refusing to allow the evacuation of the salient in the front around Apostolov with the Nikopol bridgehead and made it unmistakeably clear that the Dnieper much higher up around Kanev had to be held. Even any tactical moves to prepared positions at the upper course of the Ingul river north of Kirovograd were expressly forbidden. On the other hand, reinforcements were not forthcoming: the evacuation of Bayerlein's 3rd Panzer Division had already been ordered. Since even the creation of reserves from men in front-line units not expected to be involved in the initial fighting seemed impossible, the senior commanders looked towards the coming days with dread. The front was so thin it could be ripped right open.

Hitler had always underestimated Soviet strength. 'There is no longer a Soviet Army, what survives is only a police action ...' he announced in 1941. Even the subsequent course of events could not prise him free from this preconceived opinion, this wishful thinking. There is probably no doubt that at the beginning of 1944 he himself still firmly believed in final victory. And the astounding fact – which today seems almost incredible – is that he knew how to convey this belief to the world around him. It is easy enough now to shake one's head or dismiss Hitler as a fool. A fool cannot move the world. He was a demon, equipped with unique suggestive powers. His influence on people was enormous. Even the most convinced opponents of his ideas never came away from him without at least a doubt in the back of their minds: 'perhaps he's right'. It remains uncertain how much the anxious hope of the individual contributed to it. The fact itself cannot be denied and can even be read between the lines quite easily in many memoirs insofar as they can be taken seriously and are truthful.

Hitler believed that the collapse of the Soviet Union was imminent. According to him, at this stage its last divisions had finally bled out and were exhausted as a result of the heavy offensives of the past winter. Now a major offensive would strike the collapsing colossus a coup de grâce with a major offensive against Kiev originating from around Kanev–Korsun. This attack, carried out to the right along the Dnieper, would cut off and destroy anything heading westwards along the river, and be a repeat of the large encircling battles of 1941 and 1942.

This assessment of the situation, an under-estimation of the Soviet Union's forces and at the same time an over-estimation of the available German forces, resulted in orders to hold Nikopol, hold around Apostolov, hold Kirovograd and hold the bend in the front at Kanev–Korsun that was to be the springboard for the final battle in the East before the threatened invasion in France had time to materialise.

The actions of Eighth Army, 5–7 January 1944 (Maps 2, 3)

The expected Soviet major offensive began on 5 January with a devastating half-hour artillery barrage along the entire front of LII Army Corps and XXXXVII Panzer Corps. This identified two points of main effort very clearly. Zhukov's double encirclement at Stalingrad had found its adherents and become doctrine. Accordingly General Koniev (2nd Ukrainian Front) did not attack Kirovograd itself, but strove for the breakthrough north and south of the city intending to wheel inwards and create the pocket later.

To the south at Novgorodka (30 kilometres south-east of Kirovograd), 2nd Parachute Division (Lieutenant-General Rancke) defended 21 kilometres of front line with 3,200 men: to the north near Snamenka (30 kilometres north-east of Kirovograd) 10th Panzer-Grenadier Division (Lieutenant-General Schmidt) defended 18 kilometres with 3,700 men. These positions had been gained by the Germans on 31 December in counter-attacks. The grenadiers lay mostly unprotected on the frozen terrain in deep snow. Both divisions were overwhelmed. By the early afternoon Soviet tanks had positioned themselves 20 kilometres behind the front facing the corps command post in the northern outskirts of Kirovograd.

The Red breakthrough had therefore practically succeeded on the first day, the German front torn open. Large formations in reserve were not available. Yet the almost inevitable collapse did not occur. The reasons for this may be assumed to be sluggish leadership combined with poor training of troops on the Soviet side, and a desperate stopgap system with the most dedicated readiness of the individual to fight on the German side.

Corps armoured groups counter-attacked the fast Soviet units deployed for the breakthrough and particularly in the southern areas, supported by heroic nests of resistance, achieved fine local successes. It was very soon evident, however, that the Eighth Army forces were no longer sufficient to close the front. Bayerlein's 3rd Panzer Division, ready to pull out west of Kirovograd, offered to remain and was attached to Eighth Army for later deployment with XXXXVII Panzer Corps.

In the intended southern breakthrough area, the Soviet fast units – during the morning including almost 200 tanks – encountered bitter resistance from valiant battle groups and flanking attacks by 13th and 14th Panzer Division armour before reaching the river Ingul.

In the intended northern breakthrough area, however, the counter-attack by units of 11th Panzer Division against the wedge of Soviet tanks advancing to the south-west was unsuccessful. The Soviets were now threatening to encircle Kirovograd from the north and west and to bring it about by severing the supply lines.

The ferocity of the fighting is demonstrated by the destruction of 153 Soviet tanks on 5 January. Enemy losses in personnel and materials were high, those on the German side ominous in scale. For example, 10th Panzer-Grenadier Division alone lost 620 men.

The evening situation was still uncertain: despite shortening the central front line near Adshamka (376th Infantry Division and 14th Panzer Division), it could not be sealed sufficiently.

On the night of 6 January the enemy brought into the northern breakthough area a strong force of infantry, and from other fronts another five rifle divisions.

The presence of ten to eleven rifle divisions was confirmed in the southern breakthrough area, and another eleven in the northern area.

Even if these divisions had been little rested and and were composed to some extent of poorly trained men (we called them *Beutesoldaten*, 'looted soldiers'), the imbalance in the infantry ratio was at least 8:1.

In the later course of the battle, the main task of the enemy artillery was to offer flank protection, which was achieved by quickly establishing extensive and deeply echeloned anti-tank gun positions. To support the attack itself they lacked a centrally controlled fire direction system and flexibility in the creation of points of main effort. For these reasons fortunately for us their extraordinary strength was not used to the best effect. This failing may also have been caused by difficulties of supply and the nature of the roads, which hampered timely resupply of ammunition to the numerous army artillery units.

Our own artillery supported the heavy defensive fighting by concentrated fire with a high expenditure of ammunition. On 5 and 6 January, 177,000 shells were fired. This was often successful in nipping minor attacks in the bud. As a result of our high losses in infantry, at many places – especially the many gaps in the front – the artillery bore the burden of the defensive battle alone.

We deduced from the number of enemy tanks appearing on 5 January that several tank corps were participating. From prisoners we pieced together the presence of XVIII Soviet Tank Corps and VIII Soviet Mechanised Corps in the southern attack area, and VII Soviet Mechanised Corps, V Soviet Guards Mechanised Corps and an independent tank regiment in the northern attack area. Making use of the deep breaches in our lines in the northern breakthrough area, after the arrival of elements of XXIX Soviet Tank Corps around Vershina and Kamenka the enemy grouped up his fast units and transferred VIII Soviet Mechanised Corps into the northern area on the night of 5 January.

The deployment of fast units corresponded to our own principles, but in carrying out the operation the Soviets lacked flexibility in concentrating the point of main effort and were over-anxious about their flanks. A significant contributory factor was probably the local successes achieved by even our smallest indefatigable companies of panzers. Here the German panzer crews proved their superiority repeatedly. Moreover the enemy was deceived as to our own weakness in numbers by this kind of aggressive defence.

On the morning of 6 January the Soviets sent out their superior numbers of tanks for the expected encirclement of Kirovograd. Through offensive planning large numbers were pinned down at the defensive fronts. The attack by 3rd Panzer Division to seal off the gap in the northern front resulted in bitter fighting although only the hilly terrain at Roshnatovka (10 kilometres north of Kirovograd) was captured. This did not prevent VII Soviet Mechanised Corps crossing the Ingul river at Sseverinka and cutting off the big wide road to the west of Kirovograd. In the south, XVIII Soviet Tank Corps reached the outskirts of Kirovograd, the encirclement of the city appeared imminent.

The restoration of the situation east of the Ingul river was no longer possible. We had to attempt to prevent any further breakthrough at the river by intercepting it from our prepared position there. This could be done if reinforcements took on the job of wiping out the enemy elements that had already crossed the Ingul river heading west.

Reserves had been requested early on from Army Group and agreed upon. The possibilities of what the army could do were exhausted, especially since pulling back LII Army Corps had been strictly forbidden by Hitler. The corps restored the connection to Sixth Army in the pocket at Apostolov. Withdrawing XXXXVII Panzer Corps from north of Kirovograd to the Ingul river was no longer a decision the army could make independently.

Panzer-Grenadier Division Grossdeutschland, sent up by the Army Group, was expected to begin arriving on the evening of 7 January south-west of Kirovograd with orders to seal off the front there. Until then the important thing was to win time and intercept any Soviet attempt to cross the Ingul. This was the thinking behind our operations of the following days in which defensive and offensive thrusts followed in quick succession and with varying degrees of success.

Between the two Soviet breakthrough areas were three divisions, 376th Infantry Division, the remnants of 10th Panzer-Grenadier Division and 14th Panzer Division. It was decided that these could be used for the all-round fortification of Kirovograd: 14th Panzer Division would be used to seal off the gap at the southern end of the city. The same night, a heavy enemy force penetrated into the southern sector of the city and collided with the 14th Panzer Division launching position. Bitter house-to-house fighting ensued in which the Soviets succeeded in forcing their way almost to the northern end of the city. This broke up the all-round position. During the night of 7 January, 376th Infantry Division and the remnants of 10th Panzer-Grenadier Division fought their way along the west bank of the Ingul to Lelekovka where, crowded together, they found themselves initially isolated. Meanwhile 14th Panzer Division, which after the energy-sapping streetfighting had occupied a defensive position at the western edge of Kirovograd, succeeded by means of a determined attack early on 8 January in linking up with the battle group at Lelekovka.

Meanwhile VII and VIII Soviet Mechanised Corps had encircled 3rd Panzer Division north of Kirovograd. In a bold night attack, with the panzers protecting the unarmoured elements on all sides, General Bayerlein broke through the encirclement and the centre of the enemy force to reach Vladimirovka early on 8 January. Under his outstanding leadership, the division turned about and in a counter-attack to the east took Ossikovata the same afternoon. A rare example of the still unbroken fighting spirit of the troops.

South of Kirovograd the Soviets were continuing their advance. While moving up, the first groups of Panzer-Grenadier Division Großdeutschland attacked in order to bring them at least to a standstill.

The attempt to halt the enemy advance at the Ingul river failed. Only the Lelekovka battle group still held out as the last pillar of the German position in the Kirovograd area, tying down strong enemy forces and preventing the two forces that had broken through from joining up, but on both sides the front was torn open. Enemy motorised, mechanised and armoured units made their way through the gaps over the Ingul and assembled on the west bank ready to continue the breakthrough.

The crisis of the battle on 8 January 1944 (Maps 1, 3)

The great battle culminated on 8 January. Bad news came in from all sides. There was scarcely any doubt still possible: General Koniev had achieved the breakthrough.

In the southern breakthrough area at midday his tanks were already 30 kilometres south-west of Kirovograd. Between them and Pervomaisk, the Rumanian border town on the Bug river, there were no German forces in place or close enough to react.

In the centre the full encirclement of 376th Infantry Division, 10th Panzer-Grenadier Division and 14th Panzer Division around Lelekovka loomed. Hitler had given his personal order that these divisions were not to move, but maintain their position as a stronghold.

Gruskoye to the west of Lelekovka had been lost. It was clear that the VIII Soviet Mechanised Corps and its infantry were preparing to advance west towards Uman. In their path the only German opposition consisted of observation posts.

To the north, 11th Panzer Division reported a major attack by VII Soviet Mechanised Corps. They did not think that in the long run they could withstand the increasing pressure.

Farther north still, 4th Soviet Guards Army was attempting to force XI Army Corps (Stemmermann) to evacuate the Dnieper Bend prematurely and by pinning-down operations prevent the release of German forces. Quiet reigned only along the Dnieper itself and at XXXXII Army Corps (Lieb) on the western front of the deep pocket.

Reports were received additionally of severe reverses suffered by the latter's western neighbour. 1st Ukrainian Front was pressing on successfully to the south, deep in the rear of Eighth Army. Shashkov, Pogrebishche and Berditschev had already fallen to them. The counter-attack by General Hube's First Panzer Army was developing haltingly. How this would make itself felt was in question.

The objective of the Soviet operations, the merging of 1st and 2nd Ukrainian Fronts in the Pervomaisk–Uman area and the onset of the catastrophe now threatened.

To avoid a second Stalingrad, the breakthrough at Kirovograd had to be halted as quickly as possible. The unified forces of Eighth Army were insufficient for a counter-attack. Various additional forces had to be brought up. The aim was if possible to pin down heavy enemy forces on the sealed fronts by stubborn resistance while containing and weakening those enemy units that had already broken through. This latter was to be achieved by panzer thrusts and small-scale attacks, the objective being to prevent the enemy advancing westwards with a large assembled force. The second task was then to erect a cohesive front as far to the east as possible.

By the evening of 8 January in the area south-west of Kirovograd, Panzer-Grenadier Division Grossdeutschland succeeded in intercepting and restraining enemy forces advancing on the flank towards Pervomaisk. Side by side with this action to the right, the gap to LII Army Corps was closed and held with a small number of soldiers in counter-attacks by elements of 3rd SS-Panzer Division Totenkopf, 13th Panzer Division and the makeshift Corps Abteilung A.

In the northern breakthough area the only formation freely available was 3rd Panzer Division, to which was given the decisive assignment to advance from Ossikovata eastwards and southwards and tie down VII and VIII Soviet Mechanised Corps. Its attacks would thereby relieve the pressure on the group trapped at Lelekovka and at the same time make it possible to draw back the divisions on the northern flank of XXXXVII Panzer Corps and XI Army Corps to the Gruskoye–Smela line.

The day that had begun so gloomy and calamitous seemed to be approaching a better end than could ever have been expected. By evening the Soviets had not set off westwards from Gruskoye, while our difficult planned withdrawal under enemy pressure had gone ahead. If we were successful soon in obtaining from Hitler freedom of action for the three divisions in Stronghold Lelekovka, it might be possible to create a unified front.

Still beset by concerns but now with a certain confidence, that night XXXXVII Panzer Corps command HQ occupied its new location in Mal-Viski on the supply route from Pervomaisk near the large Luftwaffe airfield. All reports from divisions until long after midnight sounded optimistic and good. Nowhere had there been a collapse.

During the nightly reckoning and planning towards 0200 hrs suddenly we heard rifle fire and the short, sharp double report of tank guns firing to which the airfield flak replied.

Soviet T-34 tanks rolled past our huts, the infantry carried on their decks blazing away wildly, overcoming everywhere the hastily improvised resistance. Major Hasse, corps adjutant, a gold-medal winner at the 1936 Olympics, fell while engaging the enemy as did the outstanding staff officer First Lieutenant Becker. A Corps HQ did not hold any armour-piercing weapons and there was no protection from combat troops, because these had been sent to the front-line a long time ago. The heaviest and most painful losses were suffered by the corps signals detachment.

More important than the danger to ourselves was the need to suppress exaggerated rumours that might unsettle the weak, still mobile front. We also had to establish from where the Soviet tanks had come. Our own divisions had reported immediately: everything in order. If these reports could be relied upon, the tanks must have come from the west, approximately from Shashkov and attacked at our backs. That would foreshadow the beginning of the catastrophe. Going by the latest of the reports it was very possible that the front in the west had been broken, and we had not been notified of the fact.

By daybreak, command HQ was working in the neighbouring village of Noviy Mirgorod in a borrowed army telephone exchange and aided by two salvaged radio signals posts. Once again our own divisions reported: everything in order. In the course of the morning the proceedings were clarified and the cause found to be characteristic of our immediate situation, namely the lack of strength and depth of the front.

When darkness fell, 67th Tank Brigade of VIII Soviet Mechanised Corps set out from Gruskoye southwards carrying infantry on the tanks.

The brigade had passed through the thin front and then rolled for hours across our terrain without ever being noticed. From the interrogation of prisoners it was not possible to determine whether this had been a bold but pointless thrust against Mal-Viski in order to put out of action a senior command HQ, the airfield and the railway goods yard, or the first step in the feared link-up of 2nd Ukrainian Front at Kirovograd with 1st Ukrainian Front at Shashkov. The only significant factor initially had been that the Soviet tanks had not come from the west, from Shashkov.

Mal-Viski was surrounded and the Soviet brigade wiped out with the enthusiastic cooperation of the Luftwaffe. Colonel Rudel, *the* tank-destroyer of the Luftwaffe, led Immelmann Squadron from Slinka, 30 kilometres to the south. He took part in the fighting and was credited with 16 burning Soviet tanks in the 15 missions he flew on 10 January.[1]

Eighth Army engagements 9–17 January 1944 (Maps 3 and 4)

9 January began with welcome news. The three encircled divisions at Lelekovka had been given freedom of action by Hitler.

Their situation meanwhile had greatly deteriorated. So strong had the endless enemy attacks become, supported by waves of ground-attack aircraft, that the end of the unequal struggle seemed to not be much longer in doubt. Supply from the air covered only the barest minimum of their requirements. 11th Panzer Division was so firmly tied down by superior enemy attacks that its planned relief thrust to the south had to be cancelled. Likewise elements of 3rd Panzer Division en route for Mal-Viski had also been forced to turn away. Relief and help came only from Battle Group Grenadier Regiment 331, which had been assembled west of Gruskoye. Carrying through a boldly led attack, which surprised everybody by passing through Gruskoye and winning territory to the east, the Lelekovka group broke out without losses on the night of 9 January. The same night the three divisions occupied a position ajacent to Grossdeutschland on the right hand and 3rd Panzer Division, west of Gruskoye, to the left.

---

[1] See Hans Ullrich Rudel: *Trotzdem* (*Stuka Pilot*).

The Soviets had apparently decided beforehand that nothing could be done to save the men in Stronghold Lelekovka and dropped the following leaflet on the three divisions in question which gave our men much amusement:

German Troop Units North of Kirovograd Wiped Out

According to an OKW report, German troops have broken through the northern arm of Kirovograd and have withdrawn in this direction.

In reality the events took place in the following manner:

The retreating remnants of three German panzer divisions devastatingly cut down north of Kirovograd were encircled on 9 January together with one motorised and one infantry division.

In order to avoid unnecessary bloodshed, the High Command of the Red Army offered the German troop commander the opportunity to lay down his weapons immediately.

Because this offer of capitulation was rejected by the German commander, it became necessary for the Soviet troops to go on the offensive, and the greater part of the surrounded German troop sectors fell victim.

More than 15,000 bodies of German officers and men remain on the battlefield.

The Soviets have destroyed or captured: 443 panzers, 484 guns, amongst them forty self-propelled assault guns, 363 mortars, 874 machine guns, 226 armoured scout cars, 2,982 vehicles, nineteen ammunition- and other compounds.

German officers and soldiers!

Everywhere where the troops of the German Wehrmacht attempt to stem the Soviet advance they end up encircled and wiped out.

The German Wehrmacht is equally powerless whether fighting in defence or attack.

If you do not want to fall victim to Hitler's defeat strategy, make for home at once or surrender to us.

All further resistance means your certain death.

At the centre, west of Kirovograd a cohesive front was created as a result of the overnight re-grouping on 10 January, a task requiring almost superhuman energy from the officers and men of these three divisions. Additionally they had had to install themselves in the new position first, for which no kind of preparatory work had been possible. They were by no means beautifully situated but yet everywhere the men were in the best of spirits at having escaped almost unavoidable encirclement. A few hours ago the choice seemed to lie between death and captivity – and now they were home again. Apparently against all reason they had been ordered to hold Lelekovka. They had not understood the order but obeyed it. Negotiations for capitulation as the leaflet described had never taken place. Eulogies can only darken what was achieved again by the German soldier here after almost five years of war!

The linking-up in the south to Grossdeutschland had a calming effect. The Soviets were no match for this elite division when it attacked *en masse*. Two rifle divisions and elements of several tank brigades were encircled and then wiped out. On 10 January the commanding heights of Karlovka, 15 kilometres south-west of Kirovograd, fell once more to the Germans, the portentous gap in the front there being sealed.

In the north on its own initiative the army pulled back XI Army Corps behind the Irdyn Marshes on the night of 9 January. This shortening of the line left 282nd Infantry Division free and from 10 January it stood available in reserve.

In essence it seemed that the Germans had been successful in halting the Soviet breakthrough along this approximate line: uplands south-west of Kirovograd–Gruskoye–Krassnossilka–Smela for the loss of around 30 kilometres of territory. The ferocity of the defensive struggle had caused the Soviets heavy losses. There is no doubt about this from captured papers and the statements of all prisoners under interrogation. Their fast units had been hit hard. Nevertheless after the Soviets had combined the infantry divisions of 5th Soviet Guards Army and 53rd Soviet Army and concentrated the remnants of their 5th Soviet Guards Tank Army forces, we had to assume that General Koniev would resume the effort to break through.

These expectations came to pass. On 11 January after a heavy artillery barrage the enemy set forth again from the area north of Gruskoye. His tanks were arranged into individual strong groups to precede the infantry. Our weak front was forced back, but held. The momentum of the Soviet attack faltered noticeably. Caught in artillery fire from three sides, the Soviets suffered such high casualties that they were unable to offer unified resistance to the immediate counter-attack of 3rd Panzer Division and 282nd Infantry Division brought up from reserve. The Soviets were repulsed and the new gap sealed off again. Two other offensives from Gruskoye and north of it on the 15th and 16th caused 376th Infantry

Division, 10th Panzer-Grenadier Division and 282nd Infantry Division serious crises but no breakthrough ensued. 3rd SS-Panzer Division Totenkopf, released from other duty for an approach overnight, arrived to counter-attack at first light on 16th and made the wavering front line firm.

More difficult to destroy was the deep penetration near Krassnossilka into 106th and 389th Infantry Divisions on the boundary between XXXXVII Panzer Corps (von Vormann) and XI Army Corps (Stemmermann). Here again 3rd Panzer Division was decisive. After two eventful days of fighting, by the 17th the front held together with only minor losses of territory.

Over the next few days fighting flared up here and there locally, but the big picture showed clearly that the enemy's attacking strength had been broken. The 2nd Ukrainian Front's second winter offensive with 31 rifle divisions (7th Soviet Guards Army, 5th Soviet Guards Army and 53rd Soviet Army) and also 5th Soviet Guards Tank Army against the eastern front of Eighth Army, which was ultimately intended to have encircled the entire Eighth Army in collusion with 1st Ukrainian Army after it destroyed First Panzer Army, fell short in its objective. The failure to break through accompanied by serious Soviet losses stamped the battle as a success for the bloodied survivors of the German divisions.

The course of the defensive battle was marked by:

1. Hitler's order to hold the front at all costs, which made mobile warfare impossible. It prevented large complete units becoming available to the High Command as reserves.
2. The low combat strength and their frightening losses. This made it impossible to deeply stagger the main battlefield with infantry positions so that every local penetration tore open the front and could have been used by the enemy to break through.
3. The weak stand-by reserves, mainly small groups of panzers, at the command HQs. They could weaken and halt the enemy, but not destroy him decisively.
4. The lack of any High Command reserves.

CHAPTER 3

Psychological stresses

The intention of the Soviet leadership to encircle and wipe out all Eighth Army at the beginning of January 1944 miscarried. In retrospect historians may consider this a German victory. At the time the troops at the front did not have that sensation. There was no victorious talk of any kind. The heavy fighting in temperatures as low as minus 30°C had literally asked the utmost of every man. Because the available forces were never sufficient to seal off the gaps in the line if it required action against the enemy in order to do so, and the defences had not been staggered in echelons immediately behind the main battle line, every enemy intrusion meant that the adjoining troops also had to be pulled back. Even if that meant only by a few hundred metres, the infantrymen in particular had to dig new positions in ice and snow while exposed to the Russian winter and enemy fire. There are no words that can do justice to the achievements of the German soldier on the Eastern Front!

To this psychological overstrain came doubts. By the beginning of 1944 no individual can have remained unassailed by them.

Despairing hope and the sense of duty struggled against common knowledge and shrinking confidence in the 'Führer'. The orders from above seemed increasingly incomprehensible and apparently more senseless.

Did we at the front really understand the overall situation correctly? Were we not drawing false conclusions as to the whole from our small sector of visibility? Hadn't we capitulated in 1918 only five minutes before the gates shut?

Was there any getting out of the boat in which we were all sitting? When all was said and done, wasn't Hitler the only man who alone could still save Germany? Was there still some point in risking one's life for a cause which looked lost? Were we still bound by the Soldier's Oath when things looked really bad?

How the German soldier came to terms with all these doubts and how he answered the questions is exemplified by his behaviour at the front. And how the German people thought was reflected by the overwhelming majority condemning the 20 July plot at that time. The many thousands who discovered after the collapse that they had 'always been against' the regime, had always been Resistance fighters, did not consider it expedient to bare their whole hearts to humanity in 1944.

The soldiers at the front kept faith with each other and with Germany. Later the 1945'ers emptied buckets of filth over them. A too cheap, too transparent attempt to transform true values for personal use and a longer life.

But it was made hard, very hard, for the German soldier of that time not to be led astray. While the Western Powers with their absurd demand for unconditional surrender swept aside from the very beginning any possibility of negotiated peace, Stalin made masterly use of the situation. Skilfully staged, just at the right psychological moment, the National Committee Free Germany (*Nationalkomitee Freies Deutschland*) and the League of German Officers (*Bund Deutscher Offiziere*) made their bow to an astonished world.

Their basis was Stalin's order to the Army of 23 February 1942 which included the phrase: '... Hitlers come and go, but the German Volk, the German State, remains,' and his solemn declaration on 6 November 1942 with this programme:

> The overthrow of racial exclusivity, equal rights of nations, inviolability of their territories, liberation of the oppressed nations, restoration of their rights of sovereignty, the right of every nation to set itself up as according to its own wishes, economic aid for all nations which have suffered damage, support for the same in achieving their material welfare, restoration of the democratic freedoms, destruction of the Hitler regime.

The propaganda became ever more stirring, appealing to heart and mind at the same time, pulling out all the stops. It began by reciting centuries-old peaceful cooperation and brotherhood in arms, proceeded to Yorck's decisive act at Tauroggen in 1812, Bismarck's political legacy, the 1922 Treaty of Rapallo, the friendship of Seeckt, the Moscow Accord of 1939 – nothing was forgotten. Peace and friendship were guaranteed and it all hinged on just one condition: immediate surrender.

Grand old Prussian military names, pregnant with tradition, were resplendent amongst the thousands of leaflets that flooded the front. Agents with carefully forged documents of identity, loudspeaker vans and transmitters in the Soviet trenches called everywhere to the troops to desert, refuse orders, mutiny. One of the loudspeaker speeches of Graf von Einsiedel, a great-grandson of Bismarck, is an example which runs as follows:

German Officers and Soldiers!
The fate of the nation lies in your hands. Reflect upon the fact that with every day longer the war lasts, Hitler leads Germany deeper into catastrophe. Do not let yourselves be fobbed off any longer by the empty promises of unscrupulous exploiters. The continuation of the war can no longer change the fate of the Hitler regime, it leads to the destruction of our Fatherland.

Comrades!
You know the situation but ask yourselves, what can the individual do to change it. Comrades, you individuals are an army of millions! The world's three Great Powers cannot defeat you. But you are a powerful force if you organise yourselves against Germany's true enemy, against Hitler.

Organisation of Front soldiers! Organisation against Hitler in all Wehrmacht units and ranks. Against Hitler! In many divisions, far-sighted and courageous comrades have joined illegal groups of the movement *Freies Deutschland* and have made contact with us across the front. Follow their example! Organise yourselves into small groups and fight for our solutions:

The removal of Hitler by the Army!
Orderly retreat to the Reich frontiers!
Conclusion of an immediate armistice!

Often a word of skilful criticism can open a comrade's eyes. Work illegally until you have won over your unit. From the individual to the group. From the group to the troop. That is how the uprising against Hitler is to be prepared. You may be sure that there are sufficient determined men amongst the generals who will act when they know they have the troops at the front on their side. Every individual can and must act today!

Comrades!

Forwards for a free and peaceful Germany![2]

These were the same tones which had rung across Germany in 1918. On the new gramophone record the only difference was Hitler for Kaiser Wilhelm. Primitive and banal though the process may strike one as being, its effort to drive a wedge between the Leader and the Led brought in its train an enormous emotional burden. Hitler himself had prepared the ground for it. All responsibility lay exclusively with him, therefore in the last analysis all guilt.

The constant repetition of all failings and omissions recorded in valid legal form by known personalities from captivity and emigrées: the foreign radio stations, which naturally despite the ban were listened to: official enemy armed forces reports and detailed reports on misfortunes only admitted in a camouflaged form: fly-posters and loudspeakers, rumours about sabotage, betrayal, misappropriations, even crimes by the leading personalities, skilfully spread secretly from mouth to mouth, were not without effect in the long run. Self-conscious, smiling non-acceptance at the beginning was followed by doubt and then often enough despair and breakdown.

The tensions that had existed all along between Hitler and the Army were known, used and enlarged. Since 1941 the 'Führer' had not only been Supreme Commander of the Wehrmacht, but also officially Commander-in-Chief of the Army. In contrast to the Kriegsmarine, Luftwaffe and SS, there was therefore no man who had the special confidence of the Army and bore responsibility towards it for whatever happened.

Out of mistrust and suspicion there followed in due course the step which practically removed the Army's head and replaced it with that of Hitler. It was hardly realised at the time that by his taking over this office, Hitler's actions and orders from the mysterious darkness of the political machinery and high strategy would intrude into the area of the simple soldier's competence, since he had to suffer its consequences personally. The criticism now was that the measures Hitler took as Commander-in-Chief of the Army would automatically draw into their

---

[2] Heinrich Graf von Einsiedel, *Tagebuch der Versuchung*, Pontes Verlag, 1950.

circle his activity as Supreme Commander of the Wehrmacht, Leader of the NSDAP and Head of State.

The defeat of the U-boats in the Atlantic and the failure of the Luftwaffe especially to protect the skies over the homeland were matters for the Supreme Commander of the Wehrmacht. The letters that arrived at the front brought no good news and had a softening - up effect on the will to fight with their reports of distress, the bombing terror, the behaviour of the party bigwigs and the activities of the Gestapo.

Despite it all, it must be stated to the honour of the German soldier that he bore even these burdens. Enemy propaganda had no tangible success. The sense of duty, loyalty and the soldier's oath proved stronger. There was never a single incident of abandoning arms or mutiny, and the number of defectors was so insignificant as to not be worth the mention. However doubts grew. It is more difficult to die with doubt in the breast than with confidence in victory, for ... 'everybody wavers where belief is absent.'

One must therefore laud the achievements which German soldiers accomplished despite all the difficulties, and the bearing with which they later bore their fate.

When their confidence in the Führer wavered, nevertheless their belief in the German Volk and Germany remained unshakable. They believed that loyalty is repaid with loyalty. Until *their* world collapsed in May 1945.

> 'Trust, belief, hope is gone,
> For they all lied to me, whom I had highly revered:
> Deceit is everywhere and hypocrisy,
> And murder and poison and perjury and betrayal.'

From Schiller: *Wallenstein's Death*, 7th Act.

By that, even Max Piccolomini did not mean only his idolised leader Wallenstein.

CHAPTER 4

In expectation of the new attack
17–25 January 1944 (Maps 1, 4, 5)

Officers and men at the front were exposed to a surfeit of worries of all kinds at that time. From 6 January the official OKW communiques mentioned the name Kirovograd every day, and always in connection with heavy fighting. When in the course of the next few weeks the names of the locations were changed to 'south-west of Cherkassy', 'south-east of Byelaya Zerkov' or 'east of Shashkov', it always meant Eighth Army and always still in the same location. Attack was followed by counter-attack, there was no rest, no chance of recovery for the battered divisions. It was a war of attrition at the place where it could be expected with deadly certainty that the Soviets were not going to give up after the failure of their first major attempt at encirclement. We knew well their way of going about things.

Often their divisions had been badly hit, almost wiped out, but always in a short time they bounced back. If only cadre personnel survived, that was sufficient. The supply of personnel seemed inexhaustible and they were quickly brought forward. Additionally men and women from the recently cleared territories, forcibly recruited and given odd bits of uniform to make them look military, would be found charging our lines a few days later. Who cared about their lack of training and improbably enormous losses if some of the mass, roaring up like a floodtide, somehow battered down the weak dam! The lives of people in Asia are cheap and have never counted for much. Much more important were the materials that came flowing in as the contributions by the United States and Great Britain to the eradication of the occidental culture. Stalin was still then harmless, good old Uncle Joe!

The question which the German commanders had to consider was not *if* the Soviets would persist with their attempts to break through, but only *when* and *where* he would commit his main force. Neither of the latter was very difficult to answer. Judging by all our experiences and the nature of their battle objectives of the time, namely attacks aimed at pinning us down, we were looking at a restricted area of territory. Everything pointed to a transfer of the Soviet centre of effort from Kirovograd farther north.

The overall situation had undergone a fundamental change. To the west, First Panzer Army had finally gone over to the counter-attack. They had not managed to capture Shashkov and Berditschev, but at least Vinniza had been relieved and the threatened breakthrough to Uman and the Bug river prevented. The wavering front had been consolidated once again and the encirclement of all Eighth Army avoided. It could therefore be accepted that the Soviet commanders would adapt their original plan to the new situation and accordingly limit their objectives. This seemed confirmed by the major attack of 15 January to one side of the former main battle front near Krassnossilka which was regarded as a reconnaissance thrust and evaluated accordingly.

In any case, the German commanders settled for this explanation and were proved right. That ultimately they had no success is another matter.

The first priority was to create reserves quickly and place them behind the presumed threatened sector. With minor adjustments to the front, 11th and 14th Panzer Divisions had been withdrawn by 22 January and assembled as the reserve attached to XXXXVII Panzer Corps (von Vormann) around Noviy Mirgorod and Panchevo. In doing this it had to be taken into account that the already too long, over-extended frontage of the infantry divisions would be lengthened. 3rd Panzer Division near Krassnossilka itself could not be released. It was already involved in heavy fighting where the new breakthrough attempt was expected. The mass of the corps artillery was brought into position at its rear in support.

The available forces were not permitted to do anything else, for Hitler had as before forbidden a withdrawal by XI Army Corps (Stemmermann) and XXXXII Army Corps (Lieb) from the Dnieper. He was sticking to his greater plan. Therefore the only possible and reasonable solution had to be discounted and the Soviets would not do Eighth Army the favour of closing the pocket themselves. Even the withdrawal of the XI Corps eastern front line behind the Irdyn Marshes on 9 January, releasing 282nd Infantry Division, gave rise to criticism and sharp disapprobation at Führer HQ.

CHAPTER 5

The encirclement of XI Army Corps (Stemmermann) and XXXXII Army Corps (Lieb)

The breakthrough of the front in the east and west on 28 January 1944

A bold reconnaissance thrust by 3rd Panzer Division across the watery sector of Krassnossilka eastwards on 24 January, in combination with the results of air reconnaissance, dispelled the last doubts as to where the next Soviet attack was to be expected. 3rd Panzer Division had driven into the centre of the enemy launch position. The heavy artillery barrage early on 25 January therefore came as no surprise. Soon afterwards, the Soviet infantry attack was met by the concentrated fire of the very heavy German artillery presence. In vain Koniev attempted to pull out his prostrated 4th Soviet Guards Army infantry (Galanin) by the premature use of 5th Soviet Guards Tank Army (Rotmistrov). After the loss of thirty tanks this advance also stalled.

The German heavy anti-tank guns and especially the long guns of the new Panthers showed themselves to be clearly superior in this tank clash. The T-34 was vulnerable to both at all ranges visible in the optics. Satisfaction at this success of German heavy weapons at XXXXVII Panzer Corps (von Vormann) gave way to gloom in the evening when the right flank of 389th Infantry Division (XI Army Corps) was forced to avoid by diverting to Pastorskoye and Yekaterinovka. The northern flank of 3rd Panzer Division swept through without making contact.

On 26 January, 11th and 14th Panzer Divisions closed the gap at Kapitanovka in an advance to the north. This was certainly a success but could only be exploited if infantry took over quickly from both panzer divisions, because they were not suited to holding a position. A panzer-grenadier regiment at that time consisted of at most 250 to 300 men who could barely maintain observation on a section of front line 8–10 kilometres long, and certainly not occupy and hold it.

Repeatedly since 1943 the panzer divisions in the East had been given this task for which they had not been intended and were unsuitable. The panzers had been conceived as a pure weapon of attack, and had been put into formations which corresponded with the purpose. Their strength lay exclusively in attack, in mobility, not on the defensive. The strength of a panzer-grenadier regiment – two in every division after the restructuring – was specified at around 1,200 men. In 1944 the actual complement was barely 50–60 per cent of that, which included the drivers and all the rearward services. On the pure numbers count therefore, a panzer division had about the same strength as a war-establishment infantry battalion.

That was also a consequence of the commonplace intoxication with figures in the Third Reich. At the time of the great restructuring, one division would be split into two because two flags on the big map looked better than one. And then, despite all the representations at the front and the General Staff, Hitler went a step further. Instead of reinforcing the old proven units at least to some extent with men and materials, he preferred to create more and more new divisions in the Reich. It looked and sounded better, but at the same time masked the true size of the army. The highly experienced but burnt-out cadres remained at the front, a great waste with no corresponding useful effect, while the new formations were not capable of being welded into usable units until their training was paid for. This cost so much that only the cadre remained available to fight and then the game was repeated in the homeland. A panzer division in battle was an elaborate mechanism in which the individual parts came together only with difficulty and had to run smoothly. It was impossible to convince Hitler of this.

On the night of 27 January, XI Army Corps (Stemmermann) pulled back its eastern front line freeing 57th Infantry Division (Major-General Trowitz) at Smela. The attempt to provide the Kapitanovka sector with the help it needed by its immediate intervention came too late.

Without regard to casualties – in the truest sense of the word – around noon the Red masses, under fire from all the guns of 3rd, 11th and 14th Panzer Divisions, and the very strong German artillery, flooded past them heading westwards. A stupefying scene, heart-rending in its drama. No other comparison can be made: the dam was broken and the great endless flood poured into the plain, past the panzers which, surrounded by a few grenadiers, projected like rocks in the surf. Our surprise knew no bounds when in the afternoon cavalry units came galloping through our barrier fire to the west. A long forgotten, seemingly improbable spectacle. This was V Soviet Guards Cavalry Corps under Selimanov with 11th, 12th and 63rd Cavalry Divisions.

The catastrophe was clearly foreshadowed when the rumours of a major breakthrough to the west at XXXXII and VII Army Corps were confirmed. The 27th Soviet Army and 6th Soviet Tank Army (Bogdanov) had arrived either side of Boyarka on the Gniloi Tikich, a small but very deep river which would later play a fateful role at Lissyanka. 88th and 198th Infantry Divisions positioned either side of the river without any depth in the field were crushed, Boyarka and Medvin were lost on the 26th. This tore open the front and there were no reserves available to seal the breach.

The Soviet divisions continued to the east unopposed and into the backs of XI Panzer Corps (Stemmermann) and XXXXVII Panzer Corps (von Vormann). The absolute end now seemed only a matter of time which could be easily calculated. As the crow flies, the distance from Boyarka to Kapitanovka is 100 kilometres.

Eighth Army had its hands tied. The strict power of command concentrated in Hitler gave the commander-in-chief of an army very little freedom of manouevre in 1944. The Führer determined the battlefield, the operations and the deployment of the individual divisions. The high standard of signals technology made it possible for him at any time to make enquiries and intervene directly from Führer HQ in East Prussia with the corps and even smaller units.

The obvious order now, namely to liberate from the bend in the Dnieper XI Corps (Stemmermann) and XXXXII Corps (Lieb) for an attack to the south, lay beyond the jurisdiction of General Wöhler. According to one of the 'Fundamental Orders', whenever the front was pulled back, no matter by how little, the personal approval of the Führer had to be obtained *beforehand*. The decision had to be requested through channels and the response awaited. Until it arrived, the only thing which could be done was attempt to seal off the breach somewhere.

To the west near Boyarka, no forces were on hand. To the east 3rd, 11th and 14th Panzer Divisions were favourably placed. Before first light on the morning of 28 January, these three panzer divisions advanced on the northern flank of XXXXVII Panzer Corps (von Vormann) northwards for Kapitanovka. There was nothing they could do to prevent the Soviets widening the breach. The Soviets had meanwhile brought up from the south elements of 53rd Army (Managarov) from the Kirovograd area and from the north elements of 52nd Army from the Cherkassy–Smeal area. It weakened their other fronts but this was not risky as they had no fear of a German attack at either.

Where one side is either forced or goes voluntarily onto the passive defence merely to protect the territory it holds, there is no skill involved in what the other side has to do next. They have simply to assemble as many men and weapons as possible and attack. Their success is just a matter of time. The defender will be obliged to pull back: whoever in the vast expanses of the East is at a disadvantage has no hope.

'*Whoever defends in Russia – must lose*' cannot be written large enough in every manual of strategy.

The Soviet leadership (Maps 1, 5)

5th Soviet Guards Tank Army (Rotmistrov) and 6th Soviet Tank Army (Bogdanov) met up at Svenigorodka on the evening of 28 January. This completed the encirclement of XI (Stemmermann) and XXXXII (Lieb)

Army Corps with 389th, 57th, 72nd, 88th Infantry Divisions, Corps Abteilung (detachment) B, SS-Panzer Division Wiking and SS-Volunteer Brigade Wallonien, in addition to which the German front had been torn apart over 100 kilometres. The way to Rumania via Uman and the Bug river now lay open. No German units were here or within reach.

Why the Soviet leadership did not use this unique opportunity to wipe out Army Group von Manstein will probably never be explained. The only man who knew besides Stalin and his military adviser Marshal Shaposhnikov was probably Koniev as commander-in-chief of 2nd Ukrainian Front. Objective explanations cannot be expected from these sources.

All that is left for us is guesswork. Either the Soviet marshals over-estimated the available German forces, or they shrank back in horror from really wide-reaching operations. The first is hardly likely, given the well-organised Soviet intelligence service, which began immediately behind our lines and found a superabundance of political supporters worldwide.

For the same reason one cannot accept that the Soviets were unaware of the disappearance of a 100-kilometre section of the German front. The Soviet commanders on the spot must have been informed by the local inhabitants at the latest by 28 January. Colonel Kyrill D. Kalinov, who later defected to the West, described in his book *Sowjetmarschälle haben das Wort*:

> The partisans were ultimately in a position to form infantry units. Thus the tank corps of Rotmistrov and Bogdanov were accompanied by such partisan-infantry.
>
> The waves of our tanks frequently advanced so fast that the infantry could not keep up. Koniev therefore contacted Bielov, who was in charge of guerrilla warfare in the area of the Dnieper and the East Wall, and the two of them agreed that our tanks would receive support from the partisan detachments of the local area. In this way we had at our disposal infantry units stationed locally which freed our motorised units. This was an enormous relief for our system of transportation.
>
> On the occasion of the battle at Kanev, 43rd, 76th and 2nd Autonomous Partisan Brigades took part in the capture of Komarovka and Dshurdshent. They are credited with wiping out the Eighth German Army General Staff.[3]

---

[3] Hansa Verlag Josef Toth, Hamburg 1950, pp.280.

The alleged wiping out of Eighth Army General Staff, positioned at Novo Ukrainka, a good 100 kilometres farther south, and whose chief was Lieutenant-General Speidel, is a figment of Colonel Kalinov's imagination. The fact is, however, that partisan activity did flare up in unusual proportions. The still empty and abandoned villages repopulated themselves in a strange manner, and traffic was set up over which we had no longer any control. We did not even have sufficient forces to erect the most simple barrier between our own hinterland and the Soviet troops. In what may be considered to some extent 'normal times' when something happened at our front, it tended to percolate through to 'over there' anyway, and so now there was no obstacle at all.

What must be presumed is the enemy's knowledge of the distribution of our forces. Perhaps and probably the picture was darkened by exaggerated reports of fighting and successes by troop commanders. Reliable Soviet sources are not available and one assumes they never will be. General Staff Colonel Kalinov continued in the Foreword to his book:

> Before leaving my country I made a solemn promise to myself to commit to paper, simply and objectively, what I heard from the mouths of those men who in the truest sense of the word forged victory over the Third Reich. They are themselves forbidden to present witness of their deeds.

In his chapter 'Ivan S. Koniev, Marshal of the Stud Farms, Duke of Kanev', he writes about this period and quotes verbatim a series of conversations from the beginning of February 1944:

> On 3 February the Upvosso train arrived at Romodan station. It had cost much effort to get it here from Kiev, but finally it succeeded. The principal line Romodan-Kiev had been converted to the Russian gauge with astounding rapidity. Koniev, Rotmistrov, Bogdanov and Selimanov were able to reach the Ukrainian capital with their General Staffs a few days later.
>
> I heard the latest news from Colonel Kvatch, commandant of the train:
>
> 'The German Eighth Army under General Wöhler is in the Kanev Pocket. It embraces no less than nine of the best motorised divisions of the German Wehrmacht, a Waffen-SS division, namely Wiking and the motorised SS-Brigade Wallonien.
>
> 'A fresh Stalingrad is in preparation, but there is still one difficulty to be overcome, namely the Panzer Corps under Hube. This is positioned like a strongly balled and extremely mobile fist right on the edge of the pocket and could force it open.'

On 6 February, Koniev arrived at Romodan with his full General Staff. He greeted me and said, 'It is good that I meet you here, Comrade Kalinov.' I have never forgotten the conversation we had then at Kharkov. 'This time we have them. I am containing the Germans in a pincer and will not allow them to escape me again. Rotmistrov and Bogdanov have met up at Svenigorodka and hermetically sealed the pocket. Selimanov is with his Cossacks in the centre. Our cavalry is the only mobile force in the mud. The Germans cannot move, particularly not to the side where Hube is trying to get them free. Only their medium panzers are still capable of movement in these ground conditions. We outnumber their panzers fourfold. The Cossacks have developed into true panzer-crackers. They have achieved the best results with the bazookas we have supplied to them. We have mainly Kuban Cossacks deployed here while Don Cossacks are at Kalinovski.'

'Are you absolutely certain, Comrade General, that Wöhler is unable to break out of the encirclement?'

'Absolutely. There is no possible doubt,' interrupted Salomachin. 'The German hedgehog all-round defences within the pocket at Korsun-Shevchenkovskiy, Gorodishche, Mielka and Barthino were wiped out yesterday, and the entire Pocket is divided up like a fan of five blades, each totally insulated from the next. We have our T-34s and light artillery present to protect the flanks, and these are not put off by mud.'

Apart from the incorrect details about the splitting-up of the pocket, probably based on exaggerations at troop level and not corresponding to the facts, from the above we have Koniev's point of view which is important when otherwise one has only guesswork and inference to go by.

From the quote, Koniev believed that all Eighth Army including the commander-in-chief, ten divisions and a brigade had been encircled. He therefore overestimated his great success and thought that the gap still open was larger than it it actually was. For the timid and faint-hearted Soviet leadership there is neither explanation nor apology. It may be that the Red marshals, despite all the big talk, simply did not believe in the possibility of a devastating victory, they remained too haunted by the memories of past years. The mythical belief in the invincibility of the German Army was momentarily still alive and helped here to push the end a little farther away. We must leave the question unanswered as to whether that was in our best interests or not.

Grand plans on the German side (Maps 5, 6)

The next few days showed that the Soviet leadership had not seized their great opportunity and had contented themselves for the time being with the partial success. Forays by 11th and 14th Panzer Divisions from Noviy Mirgorod towards Lebedin and Shpola came across only one opponent, who went on the defensive without being confronted. Thankfully the Soviet commander of pioneers at Shpola confirmed our own reconnaissance results by his continuous radio reports regarding the laying of minefields south of the town. Naturally we checked these reports in the field and found that they were often exaggerated, but on the whole they showed without doubt a transition to the defence.

This loose chatter and bragging by the Soviet pioneers relieved us of much anxiety. Where systematic minefields of that kind are being laid, there is not going to be an advance. This made our difficult decision to extend the length of our front easier. It was necessary in order to release forces to close the 100-kilometre breach and carry out the orders issued from above.

Hitler's orders were difficult to harmonise with the situation as we saw it locally. They ordered the assembly of strong panzer forces on the inner wings of Eighth Army and First Panzer Army in order to:

1. encircle by a concentric counter-attack within the Soviet encirclement those enemy forces which had broken through,
2. destroy them,
3. restore contact between both armies within the pocket,
4. from the resulting weakening of the enemy create the pre-conditions for wide-ranging operations.

According to that, the encircled XI Corps (Stemmermann) and XXXXII Corps (Lieb) had to hold all the former positions in the Korsun Bend. It was more than bewildering! The heavy fighting, the events of the past few weeks, which had often enough brought the front to within a hair's breadth of collapse, were simply negated. Hitler's wishful thinking of a major offensive from around Kanev along the Dnieper to Kiev was therefore still alive!

Was what seemed to us impossible achievable? Were we at the front so engrossed in our everyday cares and woes that we misunderstood so fundamentally the overall situation?

Once again, apparently better judgement and perception were required to prevail against trust and duty in our own breast. But all that mattered for us was the simple fact that 50,000 of our comrades were bottled up. We had to liberate them. They had the choice of death or captivity. And captivity in Soviet hands was a fate worse than death. The Germans knew that in 1944, the British and Americans not until the beginning of the peace talks in Korea in 1952, or so they said. There was no possibility of a breakout, because it was not humanly possible. All thinking ended at: 50,000 of our comrades are in despair. How can I help?

Army Group South had envisaged the beginning of the major offensive for the 2nd, at the latest 3 February. By then the following force was to have been assembled:

1. Behind the eastern flank of First Panzer Army in the area north of Uman, III Panzer Corps (Breith) with 1st, 16th and 17th Panzer Divisions and the SS-Leibstandarte Adolf Hitler.
2. On the west flank of Eighth Army south of Svenigorodka the 3rd, 11th, 13th, 14th and 24th Panzer Divisions of XXXXVII Panzer Corps (von Vormann).
3. At the southern edge of the pocket south of Korsun, approximately around Kvitki-Morenzy, the strongest possible battleworthy elements of the surrounded XI Corps (Stemmermann) and XXXXII Corps (Lieb).

These were unusually powerful forces for our circumstances in 1944. If these nine panzer divisions had actually been assembled and available, their deployment would undoubtedly have produced successes, perhaps even enabled us to seize the initiative in the East. Then the endless retreating would finally have come to an end. Since the failed offensive at Kursk in the summer of 1943, forces had never been available for mounting our own operations. Stubbornly holding the over-extended front dominated everything.

The whole grand plan existed initially only on paper. For at least five or six days the Soviets held all the initiative. They could do what they liked, freely and unencumbered. How the situation would change on 3 February was uncertain.

The III Panzer Corps (Breith) panzer divisions were still advancing farther westwards between Shashkov and Pogrebishche. They were to be withdrawn and included in the line-up with 16th, 17th, SS–Leibstandarte Adolf Hitler, and 1st Panzer Division. While transferring-in they were to have from north of Novaya Greblya the protection of 198th Infantry Division (von Horn), which had been badly battered at Boyarka. Up to 27 January their front had been clearly facing west, now they had wheeled round towards the north.

XXXXVII Panzer Corps (von Vormann) had at first to set up a new northern front 60 kilometres long between Kapitanovka and Svenigorodka from nothing so as to release at the same time 3rd, 11th, and 14th Panzer Divisions. 13th Panzer Division was fighting within the framework of LII Army Corps south-east of Kirovograd. 24th Panzer Division was moving up from Sixth Army in the area around Apostolov. It was the only fully battle-worthy panzer division joining XXXXVII Panzer Corps, the other four panzer divisions, as the result of unceasing operations for many months, should be regarded at best as armoured battle groups.

If this grand plan was to be put into effect, it was essential that XI and XXXXII Army Corps occupied the whole bend in the Dnieper above Kanev to comply with the framework of Hitler's operational intention to advance to Kiev. Initially therefore the pocket needed a sufficient occupying force for peripheral points backed up by strong local reserves behind them in order to repel incursions. The danger of splintering into many small parts was great. By well-proven precedents the enemy would certainly strive towards this goal.

It was therefore not likely that really substantial forces could be brought together from within the encirclement for an advance on Kiev. Additionally, Kvitki and Morenzy were already held by the Soviets.

CHAPTER 6

The relief attacks

Initially no infantry units were available for the creation of the new Eighth Army Front between Kapitanovka and Svenigorodka. It appeared to be impossible to release them from the old eastern front between Kirovograd and Kapitanovka. Up to now the divisional sectors for a lasting defensive line were much too long. If they were extended any farther, the result could hardly be called a front. What then remained would be described at best as a security force perhaps able to fight off reconnaissance raids but certainly not a planned attack. The local commanders were in no doubt of that fact.

Despite that the line underwent minor straightening allowing 320th and 376th Infantry Divisions, later 106th and 2nd Infantry Divisions to be pulled out one after another and moved up northwards to Noviy Mirgorod in order to release 3rd, 11th, and 14th Panzer Divisions for the envisaged major offensive.

These difficult movements took place during the night of 28 January. They were covered on the 29th and 30th by 11th and 14th Panzer Division attacks made from Noviy Mirgorod north-west to the Lebedin area which tied down strong elements of the XX and XXIX Soviet Tank Corps.

No matter how dangerous the risk involved, all possibilities open to the German commanders were employed. Had the Soviets shown any initiative and simply marched their hordes to the south, all would have been in vain, but they remained passive until 4 February and limited themselves incomprehensibly to defending against an absent enemy. It was only possible for that reason, after the arrival of 320th Infantry Division in the Kapitanovka area, to release the first elements of 11th Panzer Division westwards as far as the region south of Shpola. Just to the south of this, and marching from Kirowograd, the 13 Tank Division reached Nadlak on 31.1.

Without awaiting the arrival of other forces, Eighth Army ordered these two panzer divisions to attack to the north through the Shpola sector. The idea was to break through the not yet firmly established Soviet front to link up with XI Corps (Stemmermann) engaged in heavy fighting around Vyasovok and Olshana. Even if this attack were unsuccessful – a possibility taken into account – the two divisions would at least tie down strong enemy forces.

Under very difficult conditions a bridgehead was erected on 1 February at Iskrennoye (ten kilomtres west of Shpola) which captured the attentions of the XXIX and XVIII Soviet Tank Corps for three days. Sixty-two of their tanks were destroyed, the success being all the more highly rated when the defenders of the small bridgehead were found to have been at one point one panzer and eighty men after the bridge over the Shpola river collapsed as a result of the thaw.

Having rightly seen a special chance of success in the surprise appearance of two powerful attacking groups simultaneously, on its own initiative Eighth Army had anticipated the grand plan. Also intended originally to break through were: XXXXVII Panzer Corps (von Vormann) with five panzer divisions via Iskrennoye-Svenigorodka into the rear of the enemy in front of XI Corps' southern front (Stemmermann); and III Panzer Corps (Breith) with four panzer divisions from the area north of Uman via Boyarka and Medvin into the enemy's rear in front of the XXXXII Corps' southern front (Lieb).

Not until a way had been forced through to Group Stemmermann in the pocket were the two attack groups to turn towards each other and so close the pincers thus encircling the enemy forces which had broken through previously, enabling us to destroy them.

It was not something established subsequently but known at the time that in the breakthrough area between the encircled Stemmermann group on one side and Eighth Army and First Panzer Army on the other were to be found: 4th Soviet Guards Army, 27th and 53rd Soviet Armies, V Soviet Guards Cavalry Corps with three divisions, very substantial elements of 5th Soviet Guards Army from Kirovograd and 52nd Soviet Army from Cherkassy on the Dnieper.

Purely numerically, the Soviets were therefore so enormously superior that the German commanders considered the German encirclement plan an improbable proposition. Their deliberations and measures were concentrated on how to help the men in the pocket as soon as possible. The High Command however adhered firmly to their encirclement plan which inevitably led to friction and very unpleasant altercations.

General Wöhler, commander-in-chief of Eighth Army, pointed in vain to the fact that the desperate situation in the pocket grew worse hourly, and that time was not available for grandiose operations. He requested in vain that instead of sending III Panzer Corps (Breith) to the north to Boyarka–Medvin, it should go north-east to Morenzy where the encircled group could not last out much longer under the growing pressure. The knowledge of the commanders on the ground as to the distress of the two corps was the reason for the premature commencement of the attack which did not do justice to the great annihilation plan.

The correctness of the independent decision to carry out the partial attack was confirmed by the course of events on 2 February. Overnight the weather changed. The day before blizzards had howled across the frozen land – now came the thaw. The *Rasputitsa* began surprisingly early. It is the advent of the spring mud, of the total loss of ways and tracks, the period when the native peasant withdraws to his stove and never leaves his cottage. He knows the pointlessness of doing any work in the open. Under the effect of sun, rain and warm winds the very heavy, black Ukrainian soil is transformed in a day into viscous, thick mud. There are no consolidated roads. The pedestrian sinks down to the calf, after a few steps loses boots and socks, wheeled vehicles become hopelessly bogged down. Even the narrower tracks of our SPWs (*Schützenpanzerwagen*, armoured infantry carriers) were sucked off. The only means of progress was by towing vehicle or panzers which could manage at most 4–5 kilometres per hour with heavy wear and tear and fuel consumption. During the colder nights a thin layer of ice would form temporarily, often so thick that even the panzer tracks froze solid in it and had to be freed with blowlamps. The number of men reporting sick with frostbite rose rapidly, for a while even exceeding the losses due to enemy action. The infantry in particular lay unprotected in the open. Their wet uniforms froze to the body overnight. All planning, all calculations had to be abandoned. Once again the Russian climate had triumphed over the invaders.

The German soldier however was still alive and fighting. Using the night frosts, employing panzers as tractors etc., the men of 24th Panzer Division worked their way forward to Yampol like galley slaves. Their devotion to duty was exemplary. I flew over the approach road, or rather mud-bed, in a Fieseler Storch and am willing to admit that I was filled with great pride to be wearing the same uniform as the men of that magnificent division below me. At Yampol on 3 February, with justified pride Lieutenant-General Baron von Edelsheim reported the operational readiness of his men whose most advanced units had already reached Maliy Yekaterinopol. His division would bear the brunt of the coming battle early next morning heading north-east towards XI Corps (Stemmermann). The weak remnants first of all of 14th Panzer Division, then 3rd Panzer Division would follow behind, while 11th and 13th Panzer Divisions were to emerge from the recently captured bridgehead at Iskrennoye and position themselves rather later – approximately on 5 February – to their right. All the necessary orders had been distributed.

Mud had delayed the assembly of III Panzer Corps (Breith) behind the eastern flank of First Panzer Army. So far, only 16th and 17th Panzer Divisions had arrived. General Wöhler, commander-in-chief Eighth Army, made known his serious doubts regarding the possibility of reaching this distant objective with the limited forces available and over roads of deep mud. His doubts were brushed aside, as also was his request for permission to judge the development as he saw it on the ground and thus deviate the planned northward thrust of III Panzer Corps to the north-east to link up swiftly with XXXXVII Panzer Corps (von Vormann). The objective remained unchanged, III Panzer Corps (Breith) must go northwards to Boyarka-Medvin.

Thus on 3 February instead of nine there were only three panzer divisions ready for the offensive, which the cruel fates would undermine fundamentally. The force was only a third of that planned, the conditions for battle had been seriously complicated by the change in the weather, and only the objective remained unchanged as per Hitler's order. This was more than incomprehensible though by no means the worst example of how his generalship had become estranged from the situation at the front and reality.

On 2 February, 3rd Ukrainian Front (General Malinovski) had advanced from north of Apostolov to the south-west, and 4th Ukrainian Front (General Tolbuchin) had attacked Nikopol. This meant that the Soviet leaders had chosen the soft option. Instead of cutting off the large pocket with Sixth Army inside it, they had decided on a frontal assault, frittering away their strength, in order to force them out. There was still time to evacuate the totally pointless great bulge in the front by refusing to accept battle. Hitler ordered that the bulge must be held at all costs and because the available force did not extend to doing so, he ordered 24th Panzer Division to retire and rejoin Sixth Army.

All pointers, all indications to the contrary to the effect that the division was at readiness in its departure positions to move out early next morning, and that for a few days delay the deep mud would hinder more than at best a fraction of the force reaching Apostolov, were ignored. The order had to be strictly obeyed.

24th Panzer Division retraced its tracks along the same difficult route by which it had come. In the critical days it fought neither at Svenigorodka nor Apostolov. Here they had been prevented from taking decisive action, and there they arrived too late to foil the catastrophe. They dissipated their strength not in the struggle against the Soviets but in the useless battle against the mud.

The outcome of Eighth Army's major offensive was decided before the first round was fired. It had been intended originally that five panzer divisions were to have made a surprise appearance in massed formation, but not one was available south of Svenigorodka on 4 February. 11th and 13th Panzer Divisions were in action at Iskrennoye; 3rd and 14th Panzer Divisions had been pinned down again early on 4 February south of Lebedin by the powerful attacks of XXIX and XVIII Soviet Tank

Corps; 24th Panzer Division was trudging back the 300 kilometres to Apostolov from its departure position.

The fate of XI Corps (Stemmermann) and XXXXII Corps (Lieb) was therefore sealed on 4 February. All that was left now were desperate attempts to rescue the men trapped in the encirclement – against all orders.

The attack by III Panzer Corps (Breith), 4–17 February 1944 (Maps 7–11)

Despite the development of the situation, whatever thinking lay behind retaining the direction of thrust by III Panzer Corps (Breith) northwards remains a mystery. The entire advance had no aim. It might have been an inclination to believe that a corps with initially only two, at best later four panzer divisions, might be able to overwhelm five enemy armies one after the other. If that was not the thinking, the relief operation was senseless. At best it could reach Boyarka or perhaps Medvin. There it would have stood in the Soviet midst, cut off from all supply and unable to move in the deep mud: a new pocket.

Early on 4 February General Breith set off northwards with 16th Panzer Division (Major-General Back) and 17th Panzer Division (Major-General von der Medem) to the Gniloi–Tikich sector near Boyarka. The spearhead was the heavy panzer regiment commanded by Lieutenant-Colonel Baeke. Covering the eastern flank with an offensive assignment was 198th Infantry Division (Lieutenant-General von Horn), the western flank having VII Army Corps with 34th Infantry Division for protection.

This weak force soon bogged down in deep mud upon encountering increasing enemy resistance. 198th Infantry Division failed to assume its position on the east flank after leaving its departure position, and near Ryshanovka the open right flank was enveloped south of the locality by V Soviet Guards Tank Corps. East of it the tanks of XX Soviet Tank Corps thrust deep into the flank in the wide gap to Eighth Army via Maliy Yekaterinopol and threated the important rail goods yard at Talnoye. On the western side, the XI and XVI Soviet Tank Corps broke through the 34th Infantry Division security line and blocked the Rollbahn for a while. The thrust northwards came to a standstill. Artillery tractors failed, all wheeled vehicles sunk down hopelessly in the mud, fuel ran short, the supply line closed down. Supply from the air could only make up some of the shortfall.

Without waiting to assemble, one after another – as they arrived – the various groups of the Leibstandarte-SS Adolf Hitler (SS-Brigadier Wisch) and 1st Panzer Division (Major-General Koll) were thrown into the fray. They achieved the seemingly impossible, covered the flanks and restarted the advance. On 8 February, 16th Panzer Division together with elements of the Leibstandarte reached the Gniloi Tikich west of Boyarka and even forced their way across the river.

III Panzer Corps penetrated 30 kilometres deep into the enemy like a sharp wedge. To the west, the weak defences of 34th Infantry Division provided a very questionable protection: in the east, flank and rear were fully open. Another 30 kilometres separated the corps from the pocket that had meanwhile been forced around Gorodishche and Korsun-Shevchenkovskiy, at this stage due east. What had been foreseen from the outset had happened: the relief operation to the north had been a serious blunder. Blood and energy had been wasted uselessly.

In East Prussia it had been recognised that any new movement towards Medvin was pointless. III Panzer Corps received the order to abandon the advance to the north and proceed from the Vinograd area (15 kilometres south of Boyarka) to the east via Bushanka-Kissyanka (both villages on the Gniloi Tikich) to Kvitki. This was nothing more than mounting a relief operation by the direct and closest route.

Five precious days had meanwhile been lost, and the re-grouping cost us two more. The territory we had just gained with such difficulty on the Gniloi Tikich was vacated and the reinforced 16th Panzer Division pulled back to the south, an increasingly difficult undertaking under mounting enemy pressure.

General Breith led 17th and 16th Panzer Divisions as spearhead at the centre, 1st Panzer Division was to cover the southern flank in an offensive manner, the Leibstandarte-SS the north flank.

On 11 February we had a very promising success. There had been a light frost so that the ground held and apparently the new direction of our thrust took the enemy by surprise. Pressing well ahead, 1st Panzer Division took Bushanka on the Gniloi Tikich in their first approach, the 17th and 16th Panzer Divisions set up on their left hand building small bridgeheads over the river.

With that, the impetus of the first relief operation fell away. The Soviets brought up new elements of the V Soviet Guards Tank Corps. The misty winter weather prevented the Luftwaffe flying. For the same reason supplies came to a standstill, particularly fuel, which could only be supplied by air. Moreover aircraft had problems taking off from the unconsolidated and therefore deep and soft airfields in the hinterland. The Rollbahn was cut off again. Left to their own devices the panzers advanced. Their numbers sank alarmingly since recovery machines and repair materials were not available. Panzers could now win territory, but not clear and hold it, an adage as old as the panzers themselves. New resistance would flare up in the territories newly won, for the panzer-grenadiers conveyed in wheeled vehicles became bogged down in the mud far to the rear.

The XVI Soviet Tank Corps pressed forward energetically to the south, apparently heartened and stimulated by the withdrawals on 9 and 10 February. The Leibstandarte, which had to cover the ever-lengthening northern flank, gave up. Elements of 17th Panzer Division, the real spearhead, were compelled to turn back to assist.

16th Panzer Division overcame all difficulties, erected a bridge over the half-frozen Gniloi Tikich, set off to the east again on the 12th and despite being under constant threat took charge of the open northern flank at Dashukovka. 1st Panzer Division made no use of the new bridgehead at Bushanka and went south of the river towards Lissyanka. This may have been enforced tactically by the enemy, for the road did not go to the pocket at Komarovka. Lissyanka lay on the northern bank of the river, and Gniloi Tikich, only crossable on bridges, presented a considerable obstacle being twenty to thirty metres wide and the waters deeper than two metres. Ice projected far out from the soft, swampy banks: at the centre of the river large ice floes drifted in the sluggish current. Later the encircled XI and XXXXII Corps had to pay dearly for their relief on the southern bank of the sector.

There were no important successes on 13 and 14 February. 1st Panzer Division entered Lissyanka and were met by fierce resistance. 17th Panzer Division thrust out southwards from the area east of Dashukovka in a vain attempt to set up a river crossing for its neighbour, but the failed relief attempt of 12 February could not be made good. 1st Panzer Division could not cross Gniloi Tikich. On the northern flank at the same time XVI Soviet Tank Corps came from Boyarka and attacked the rear of 16th Panzer Division heading east, forcing large elements of it to turn away west and north. Despite that Lieutenant-Colonel Baeke entered Chishinzy, from where a mere ten kilometres now separated him from the encircled German units, but his force of panzers was not strong enough to hold the village against the concentrated attacks by V Soviet Guards Tank Corps and he was forced to avoid combat by heading west.

On 15 and 16 February, III Panzer Corps made another attempt to break through. Protected by 16th Panzer Division on their rear and northern flanks against Boyarka and Medvin, 1st and 17th Panzer Divisions were ordered to proceed from Lissyanka over the commanding height 239 south of Dzhurshenzy, Panzer Group Baeke via Chishinzy to Komarovka. At Lissyanka the bridge collapsed. The entire advance failed to develop and was cancelled. Too much had been asked of the troops, the material used up.

Meanwhile XI Army Corps (Stemmermann) and XXXXII Army Corps (Lieb) had been ordered to break out to the south-west on the night of 16 February. That evening the most advanced elements of III Panzer Corps had stopped at the line Lissyanka–Oktyabr–Chishinzy. To go the last ten kilometres was beyond their remaining strength. On the 17th only Lieutenant-Colonel Baeke set out, his panzers reaching height 239 south of Dzhurshenzy during the course of the day. He pinned down powerful enemy units at Potchapinzy but this was not enough to change the fate of his encircled comrades. Help had come too late and was too weak.

The advance by XXXXVII Panzer Corps (von Vormann), 4–16 February 1944 (Maps 7–11)

Eighth Army saw itself robbed of its impetus by Hitler's decision on 3 February to order 24th Panzer Division, ready to attack from Maliy Yekaterinopol, to retire and rejoin Sixth Army. From the outset, Eighth Army Command had not shared the Führer's exaggerated optimistic appraisal of the situation. They knew that a catastrophe would develop in the pocket if help did not arrive very quickly from outside. Therefore the repeated representations by the commander-in-chief, and finally his sending III Panzer Corps (Breith) by the nearest direct route. Time was of the essence, if relief did not arrive *soon*, it would come too late.

Accordingly there had to be an attack. If the forces were insufficient for a breakthrough, they could at least tie down as many enemy divisions as possible to relieve the pocket and III Panzer Corps. At the same time the new northern front had to be set up and the gap to First Panzer Army closed. Judged by sound technical principles, all of these options would have failed.

The front was already over-extended. There could be no doubt that a serious attack would collapse it. Therefore a further weakening could be chanced. That may seem illogical, but was no more illogical than the orders that had been handed down before. Moreover, there was simply no other possibility given that no reserves could be expected and to do nothing was the same as throwing in the towel.

Bringing up horse-drawn infantry divisions into the advance would not be useful. They were already bogged down in the mud without any contact with the enemy and to deploy them in the breakthrough area against the tanks of 5th Soviet Guards Tank Army and 6th Soviet Tank Army would be sheer murder under the prevailing circumstances. We mulled it over at length but saw no other way out than to weaken the infantry divisions at the front further, freeing the four panzer divisions of the Eighth Army one after the other and to amass them as far west as possible for the thrust to the north. The river Gniloi Tikich flowed from here north to south and and was the obvious border. Using the river as protection for the flank, from its eastern bank it would be possible to go via Svenigorodka to Morenzy and join up with III Panzer Corps (Breith). This was simply the plan for which 24th Panzer Division had prepared the groundwork for the relief. It was the only solution which might make possible, if not even probable, the twin tasks of setting up a new north front and relieving the pocket.

Even though an attack from the Iskrennoye bridgehead very close to the west of Shpola exploiting the success of 11th and 13th Panzer Division on 2 February could have potentially held the enemy, depriving him of his freedom to manouevre, now there was too much against it. As a *secondary* action, if launched at the same time as the originally envisaged principal advance rolled through Svenigorodka, it could be used to protect the right flank, but as an *individual* action it was unlikely to be successful. Between Iskrennoye and the pocket were V Soviet Guards Cavalry Corps and XVIII Soviet Tank Corps; around Lebedin–Shpola on the right flank XXIX Soviet Tank Corps; around Svenigorodka on the left flank XX Soviet Tank Corps. These were certainly too much for two weak German divisions. In addition, there was the fact that acting so far east, the gap to First Panzer Army could never be closed, and would remain open under constant threat. Cooperation with III Panzer Corps (Breith) in the Morenzy area from Iskrennoye was never possible. The two objectives could only be achieved coming from Svenigorodka, never from the Shpola area. Thus with a heavy heart – but probably correctly – the whole plan was discarded. It also had to be accepted that valuable time had been wasted.

At the beginning of the month the idea of sending forth the panzer divisions from their waiting positions to advance northwards, making up for the lack of strength by mobility, had probably been justified. This hope was buried after 3 February.

After the withdrawal of 24th Panzer Division there was a lack of incentive, and all movement was sucked down in the *Rasputitsa*. All planned calculations of how long journeys would take were abandoned, all times being exceeded manifold times. It was not the fault of the troops, they literally gave their all willingly. One could use one superlative after another and still not do their achievements justice. There is no yardstick to measure the suffering of a soldier who has gone for days in the open wearing the same wet clothing and plodding through mud, not to mention being under fire and severe psychological stress. Technical troops can provide some naked statistics for a possibility of comparison. Here follows a verbatim report by the Signals Detachment of XXXXVII Panzer Corps. The corps was attached to eleven divisions simultaneously.

> Panzer Corps Signal Detachment, 447.Abtg.Gef.Std., 2.2.1944. The breakdowns which occurred in the telephone network yesterday and today were caused by:

1. The major movements of motorised units (knocking down telephone poles and crushing FF cabling);
2. By artillery fire, strafing and bombing in the area Noviy Mirgorod-Arssenyevka;
3. Damp entering no longer sufficiently watertight coupling boxes for the FF cabling (fatigue of rubber seals);
4. Lack of isolation of Ukranian overhead lines not recognised until thaw.

Efforts to repair the breakdowns are being made day and night by all available staff.

The work of a Corps Signals Detachment with full peacetime complement and equipment is based on 257 kilometres of lines. At the present the Detachment is handling and maintaining 586 kilometres of lines.

At the principal exchange, on 1.2.1944 5,155 telephone connections were made. On 1.2.1944 there were Corps exchanges at Bolshaya Vyska, Martynosh, Novo Slynka, Slynka, Pleten-Tashlyk, Chmelevoye, Mokraya Kaligorka, also at the lateral communications detachment and Arko there were around 5,000 connections on 1.2.1944.

On 30 January, the withdrawal of 376th Infantry Division had been ordered. Grossdeutschland and SS-Panzer Division Totenkopf had to take on additionally their sector near Gruskoye. The length of front guarded by these two divisions was 40 kilometres.

376th Infantry Division needed four days to cover the 35 kilometres of deep mud between Bolshaya Vyska and Noviy Mirgorod. It was a Herculean task for man and horse. Their arrival made it possible to finally free 3rd and 14th Panzer Divisions at Kapitanovka. Both assembled on 3 and 4 February to the west of and around Noviy Mirgorod. Their future deployment was planned for Svenigorodka, but first the new front to the north had to be in place. So far that had not been done.

To the east Grossdeutschland and SS-Panzer Division Totenkopf, 282nd Infantry Division, 10th Panzer-Grenadier Division and 106th Infantry Division were providing the security. In the area south of Kapitanovka, 386th and 320th Infantry Divisions held the front to the north but where its western flank was to be set up had not yet been decided. Only 30 kilometres to the west, left to their own devices, 11th and 13th Panzer Divisions held the bridgehead at Iskrennoye: it was no longer possible to supply them overland and they were relying on Luftwaffe drops. From there the great uncontrolled gap around Svenigorodka–Ryshanovka extended for 60 kilometres to III Panzer Corps (Breith), whose advance towards Boyarka to the north had just got under way.

It was planned that by further weakening the eastern front, contact could be restored between 320th Infantry Division and the Iskrennoye bridgehead by removing 106th Infantry Division from the front sector at Panchevo for deployment, although this could take a few days.

Not until this reorganisation was finished could 3rd and 14th Panzer Divisions attack towards Svenigorodka; 11th and 13th Panzer Divisions were to join the attack. This seemed the only possibility still left to provide help or at least relief to our comrades in the encirclement. The very complicated plan can only be understood in that way and its execution would only be possible if the Russian military commanders committed the same errors as before by remaining inactive to the south. There was little chance of their doing so since for many days the XXIX Soviet Tank Corps at Lebedin and XX Soviet Tank Corps at Svenigorodka had not been fixed [by German troops].

On 4 February this house of cards of desperate hopes collapsed. XXIX Soviet Tank Corps left Lebedin for the south and arrived precisely at the gap between 320th Infantry Division and the Iskrennoye bridgehead. 3rd and 14th Panzer Divisions accepted the challenge and closed the front after heavy fighting. It was tactically a victory but from the operational point of view a failure, for the two panzer divisions had to remain there shoring up the front for many days. Not until 11 February could 106th Infantry Division release 14th Panzer Division. The thrust of XXIX Soviet Tank Corps, to which XVIII Soviet Tank Corps very soon attached itself, produced an ominous threat although neither achieved anything on the battlefield itself. Fortunately XX Soviet Tank Corps around Svenigorodka remained passive.

In the feverish search for fresh possibilities to help the encircled group, Eighth Army did not even shrink back from setting up units of leave takers. At Yampol by 10 February General Haack had assembled units of two regiments' strength and attached them to XXXXVII Panzer Corps (von Vormann).

Leave-taker units were Hitler's purely personal invention. They were hated and feared. Leave takers were removed from the trains taking them home if trouble flared up somewhere, attached to units that had been given the proud name of 'company' and 'battalion' and were then tossed back into the fray. The officer did not know his men, the men were strangers to each other. There were no provisions, there was often not enough time to draw up a personnel roster. Thousands of men fell and could only be recorded as 'missing' by their units. The whole thing was diabolical, an idea produced by a brain which never understood what it was to be a soldier.

Only a *unit* of men fight, i.e. a community whose members are inwardly bound as a team. Officers and men must be welded to the death in trust and comradeship. The knowledge that one can rely on the other is the precondition for all battle-readiness of the individual, and for all achievement on the field of battle. The soldier fights only in *his* battalion, in *his* company, only there do name, honour, tradition bind him to his duty, help him to overcome his inner self, risk his life and those of his comrades at his side for an idea. This *esprit de corps* grows slowly, requires time to mature, demands of officers and men much proof of worth. Leave-taker units were not troop units but armed mobs. Their fighting strength was minimal, their bitterness and despair undermined morale and never did they ever achieve anything approaching something worthwhile to justify this squander. The very existence of leave-taker units was a crime, a deception, aimed at placing a tiny flag on a situation map where nothing actually was. There was probably no single thing which highlighted more flagrantly the chasm which had opened between front and Führer in the course of the years than the mindless, pig-headed order: 'Hold the ground at all costs'.

It may be understandable from the foregoing that no matter what emergency had arisen, the use of Group Haack as an attacking unit was never considered. Comradeship and soldierly responsibility pressured us into acting to help as soon as possible – *esprit de corps* in the German Army did not end at battalion level – but every action mounted had to have at least the possibility of success within it, however vague that might be. For the responsible officers, there was no such possibility with Group Haack. Other ways had to be found, even if they required some risk and which on sober evaluation seemed unacceptable.

The Iskrennoye bridgehead had been thought of as a departure point for a thrust to cover the eastern flank of a breakthrough attempt via

Svenigorodka. That idea came to nothing once 3rd and 14th Panzer Divisions were tied down south of Lebedin for the second time on 4 February. In the most favourable of all cases Eighth Army was still in the position of drawing enemy elements away from the southern edge of the pocket and tying them down. Even that was only possible with the forces available if the building up of the north front were postponed for later development, i.e. if we shut our eyes to the danger of doing so. That is definitely not a solution that an instructor in tactics at a military academy could ever approve. When the instructor presents the problem, however, he can never portray the pressure which is placed on a commanding officer who must decide whether to attempt to help or write off 50,000 comrades in Russia. Presumably at the green table in peacetime, discounting the rendering of help would be considered the correct solution. In 1944 we never took that line in practice.

The order was given to evacuate the Iskrennoye bridgehead and abandon the leaping wedge. 14th Panzer Division had to stretch out to the west and alongside its previous task with individual posts take over the security operating an observation line. The division was not in the position to offer stubborn resistance, at best it could observe the enemy. After its serious losses in the battle of Kirovograd it had been kept out of the line and deprived of a whole regiment which after a successful counter-attack at Kapitanovka had penetrated into the pocket on 28 January. In the event of an enemy attack it was incapable of holding its sector, but it released 11th and 13th Panzer Divisions one after the other.

In an attack to the west, 11th Panzer Division recaptured Maliy Yekaterinopol, then wheeled north to Gniloi Tikich and on 13 February in company with 13th Panzer Division at Yerki forced the crossing of the Shpola river again. Any individual armoured groups and sub-battalions still available in the Army area were brought up for the purpose regardless that the defensive fronts to east and west would be lost if attacked. Their positions could not be held if attacked. Group Haack was attached to 11th Panzer Division and assumed security duties over the territory gained, mainly around Gniloi Tikich on the west-facing front.

On the evening of 12 February, the reinforced 11th Panzer Division held the heights south of Svenigorodka. A light frost had made movements easier. This was to be the last success of Eighth Army in this entire struggle, its energy was finally exhausted. In mud and frost, drizzle and snowstorm with little by way of proper rations the troops had achieved the impossible over the last few days – but now it had come to an end. Only panzers, therefore machines, were capable of carrying out offensive operations in the difficult ground. Too much had been asked of them, and msachines of which too much has been asked eventually just stop in contrast to men and animals, amongst which limits are more fluid and not so abrupt.

The wedge jutting sharply into the enemy could go no farther. Another 25 kilometres separated it from III Panzer Corps (Breith) fighting at Lissyanka, and 30 kilometres as the crow flies from the southern border of the ominously compacted pocket at Komarovka. The following report by XXXXVII Panzer Corps perhaps describes the situation best:

> Telex to AOK 8 (Eighth Army High Command), 15 Febr. 1805 hrs. The armoured attack group consisted of Panzer Regiments 4 and 15, Panzer Abteilung 8, I/26 and Assault Gun Abteilung 911. Today it still had six panzers and three assault guns plus Assault Gun Abtg. 228 with one assault gun at Group Haack. The number of operational panzers will fall. The supply of repaired panzers can no longer be expected because motors and spare parts are no longer available. Enemy ahead of and both sides of the attack spearhead continually strengthening, also has tanks. von Vormann.

A continuation of the attack without cover left and right amid an enemy ready to defend was no longer to be contemplated. The last possibility was the despairing efforts of XI Army Corps (Stemmermann) and XXXXII Army Corps (Lieb) to force open the encirclement from within by their own efforts. The next few days would show if the unburdening had been sufficient, if enough enemy elements had been lured away. Essentially, everything was gambled on the battleworthy formations getting out of the pocket to rejoin the German lines. If that failed, the gap in the front between Eighth Army and First Panzer Army could never be closed: the precautionary withdrawal of 376th Infantry Division at Kapitanovka and 2nd Parachute Division from its position south of Kirovograd would change nothing. Furthermore these two units were too weak numerically and would additionally arrive too late.

On the evening of 16 February, a few hours before the scheduled breakout of Group Stemmermann set for 2300 hrs, XXXXVII Panzer Corps (von Vormann) had the following formation:

The eastern front – about 50 kilometres long – was secured between Bolshaya Vyska and Kapitanovka by SS-Panzer Division Totenkopf, 10th Panzer-Grenadier Division, 282nd Infantry Division, and led by the commander of 10th Panzer-Grenadier Division as Group Schmidt. The northern front between Kapitovka and Svenigorodka around 70 kilometres long was composed of 320th and 106th Infantry Divisions, 3rd, 14th, 13th, and 11th Panzer Divisions. The western front followed the Gniloi Tikich river with Group Haack on both sides of Maliy Yekaterinopol.

376th Infantry Division was ordered to hand over the position that it had only just occupied to 282nd Infantry Division which thus had its frontage extended once again to assemble around Noviy Mirgorod. 2nd Parachute Division of LII Corps marched from Kirovograd beginning at Tichkovka (50 kilometres south of Maliy Yekaterinopol).

CHAPTER 7

In the Korsun pocket

Battle of XI Army Corps (Stemmermann) and XXXXII Army Corps (Lieb), 28 January–15 February 1944 (Maps 5–11)

When 5th Soviet Guards Tank Army (Rotmistrov) and 6th Soviet Tank Army (Bogdanov) joined up at Svenigorodka on the evening of 28 January it cut the land connection to XI and XXXXII Corps. Supplies were flown from the airfield at Korsun, signals traffic continued by radio messages. In the period from 27 January to 17 February, a total of 1,016 radio messages were made between Eighth Army and the two corps.

To what extent the officer responsible, General Stemmermann, commanding general XI Corps, had been brought up to date regarding Hitler's extensive operational plans, and especially what faith he had invested in them can no longer be determined, for General Stemmermann fell during the breakout. The orders and battle instructions that reached him, however, are known. They deserve to be preserved. There is no doubt that Hitler alone and personally was responsible for them. They do not represent a glorious page in the history of the German Army. From time immemorial the giving of orders which are practically impossible to carry out are considered to be a violation of military ethics. What was ordered here was impossible of achievement, and went beyond all human capabilities.

General Stemmermann commanding five infantry divisions and one panzer division was ordered to:

1. to occupy and hold at all costs all former positions in the Bend as the departure point for the great offensive against Kiev, i.e. a front 300 kilometres long,
2. erect a new southern front 100 kilometres long between Boyarka and Kapitovka,
3. to make ready in the Morenzy-Kvitki area strong attacking forces as a breakthrough group which would be in a position to fight their way through to III Panzer Corps (Breith) and XXXXVII Panzer Corps (von Vormann) at any given time.

How the officers and men came to terms with these orders, and what they accomplished, is so unique against all the great events in the last war that it seems appropriate to retain the course of the events on the maps. The maps were made during or immediately after the fighting. The only error which later examination identified was the assumption that 1st and 2nd Ukrainian Fronts had been involved when in fact Koniev (2nd Ukrainian Front) was the sole commander. The dividing line between the two Soviet army groups had been shifted to the west shortly before.

In order to arrive at the right laudatory appraisal of the achievements of this week, it must not be forgotten that after the *Rasputitsa* set in from 2 February, all fighting, all movements were performed in knee-deep mud and during nocturnal frosts, while by day drizzle and snowstorms alternated, fuel and ammunition were extremely short, rations and clothing totally inadequate and the removal of the wounded and sick was only possible to a very limited extent. The front line held by Group Stemmermann projected into the enemy like an egg. The theme of the egg shell can also be used for the thin perimeter, which was the only permanent fixture in the pattern. The lower end of the egg was knocked away on 28 January, exposing the whole egg to ruin, leaving unprotected the contents to access and seizure. And the Soviets attacked at once.

On 29 January his hordes to the west streamed past Medvin to Korsun and Boguslav on the Rossy, while in the east his tanks and cavalry turned north to Olshana. Reserves were not available. The spacious area within the perimeter was as good as empty. The close support and rearward services of the divisions had been combed through many times, and whoever could fight had long since found himself at the front, his job taken over by Russian/Ukrainian volunteers (*Hiwis*). The pocket which would have to be held would have to be set up first.

The most urgent thing was first to close the great gap in the south and west and create a new front here. The farther south we managed to expand it, the nearer we were to home, and the better prospect we had of relief. On the other hand it would be here that we could expect the enemy's main effort to fall. The proven tactic was to attempt to split us into many small parts. At the latest with the capture of Korsun he achieved this aim. It was the geographical centrepoint of the whole region. Furthermore, the only airfield through which all supplies were delivered was here. If we lost it, the struggle would be lost for lack of ammunition alone.

The centre of the pocket we had to build was therefore established. Its extent must stand in reasonable relationship to the available forces. It meant bearing in mind that sufficient reserves for a fighting defence must stand ready, for even minor breaches by the enemy could split us up and bring about the end. We would strive constantly for greater security by closing up in a narrow area while retaining the possibility of internal movement, but the area should not be so small as to benefit the concentric fire of the Soviet artillery. These realistic, reasoned considerations were held by the commanders of both corps ignoring all orders to the contrary from above. It would be left to Eighth Army and the Army Group to explain to Hitler later the measures taken. Self-evidently the area at the Dnieper had to be evacuated as quickly as possible.

What a short while ago had been practical, and easy to carry out without a hitch, was now done with many losses under enemy pressure and under dangerous stress. The words 'Too Late' overshadowed once more the whole endeavour.

Both corps had to take the manpower for building the new front in the west and south in battalions and smaller units from the stationary divisions. This inevitably caused the undesirable mixing together of units, welcomed with the same displeasure over the centuries as now, but there was no other way since we had no reserves and breaking up the fighting divisions would mean their withdrawal. We were also short on time, for it had been clearly recognised that the fate of Group Stemmermann would be decided in the opening days. Only if we succeeded in closing the perimeter very quickly was there a chance of getting out of it again. The dates of the announced relief attacks could not be met, for even if they began on 3 February as per plan, they would not be effective until two or three days later at best. By then our fate would have been sealed. Only very swift, determined action could bring us salvation.

In the west, the improvised Fouquet fortified line held the Rossy sector making it possible by 31 January for General Lieb to pull back the remnants of 88th Infantry Division, Corps Abteilung B and elements of 5th SS-Panzer Division Wiking to Boguslav on the Rossy, turning there to Rossava, and from Mironovka to its confluence with the Dnieper. This shortened the front by almost 100 kilometres. The units released were sent at once to advance southwards towards Morenzy–Kvitki, and forced their way into Kvitki on 2 February.

This was a most welcome and very important success which perhaps brought the scheduled closing of the southern front almost within reach.

The distance from Kvitki to Olshana is barely ten kilometres. Hastily assembled elements of XI Corps held Olshana within an encirclement. From the south-east, from Kapitanovka, Stemmermann's right flank made for Olshana pivoting around the corps command post at Vyasovok. Against all expectations the difficult withdrawal movement was successful and in competition with the Soviets, occasionally exchanging fire, succeeded in restoring a cohesive front in an bulging arc around Vyasovok from Olshana to Starosselye by the evening of 4 February.

That was the day when General Breith set out from the south with III Panzer Corps for Boyarka. This aimless 60-kilometre advance by two weak divisions northwards into the region obviously brought no relief and its immediate consequence was a noticeable reduction in Luftwaffe help, its orders being to concentrate their fighting forces ahead of III Panzer Corps, for here was where the major decision was expected to occur.

The corollary was a falling-off in supplies by air. The minimum daily delivery was reckoned at 150 tonnes. This had not been met in the opening days. It sank later to a fraction and when the Korsun airfield had to be closed on account of the weather conditions, which occurred often enough on account of fog and mud, the most urgent levels for support were not met. Aircraft had to land there because of the shortage of supply containers and parachutes. The Soviet anti-aircraft fire increased daily. Elements of at least three anti-aircraft divisions surrounded the pocket. The increasing losses in transport aircraft could no longer be made good. We wanted to make war as rich men and had sunk into bitter poverty!

Because the attack groups of III (Breith) and XXXXVII Panzer Corps (von Vormann) depended on supplies by air, a further splitting up resulted. The weak fighter and ground-attack squadrons had three areas of main effort. That was beyond their possibilities. Too much was asked of the Luftwaffe, despite exemplary personal devotion to duty by individual aircrew they could not meet the demand. Already in the opening days of February in the matter of supply a new Stalingrad threatened. The time factor became decisive in its importance. The success of the relief attacks were bound to a schedule which was constantly shortening. And III Panzer Corps (Breith) went to Byorka, 24th Panzer Division from Maliy Yekaterinopol to Apostolov to rejoin Sixth Army. That was more than the soldier at the front could understand.

The previously quoted Soviet defector General Staff Colonel Kalinov relates an experience which is alleged to have taken place on the evening of 6 February in the saloon coach of Koniev's train at Romodan.

> Salomachin (Koniev's adjutant) had been fiddling with the controls of the radio receiver and suddenly gave us a sign requesting silence. We heard a fairly deep voice making a statement in the German language in words to this effect:
>
> 'Achtung! Achtung! Achtung! Here is First Panzer Army. General Hube for the Commanding General Stemmermann. We are continuing our efforts to bring you help. We are doing everything in our power. Hold out! We are following the Führer's order unconditionally and you will be free within the next twenty-four hours. I am sending a column of Panthers towards Mokraya.'
>
> Koniev propped his chin on his hand and seemed to be slurping the words in. He licked his lips.

'I heard that already this morning,' he said. 'Hube has sent out his panzers to open a breach for Stemmermann who is stuck in the pocket at Shandorovka. He is also being sent messages in plain text for encouragement. In this way Hitler is hoping to be able to avoid having Eighth Army give up before they have fired their last round. He is fostering hope in these people and getting them to believe in a miracle. But it won't change anything. Eighth Army will suffer the same fate as Sixth Army under Paulus. That is, it will disappear completely. Nevertheless it affects me deeply to hear these calls to hold out and picture what hopes they awaken in these encircled soldiers and how they are being spurred on to desperate endeavours. Is there anything more moving than the death struggle of a mass of men such as this Eighth Army under von Stemmermann, to whom I shall be giving very soon the coup de grâce?'[4]

There is no such place as Mokraya on the map. It is also certain that Colonel-General Hube would never have agreed to broadcast that kind of rubbish on the ether. A relief within 24 hours from the situation as it stood on 6 February was an absolute impossibility, no German soldier would have believed it. Perhaps the idea was to represent Hube as a general who would try to deceive his men and was unusually stupid. He fell in 1944, and can therefore not defend himself against the slur. Perhaps his good name was used by the Soviets for their own purposes. It might be added as a marginal comment that Hube had an unusually bright, lustrous-sounding voice, not deep at all.

In addition on 6 February, the pocket was still 60 by 30 kilometres in extent and the mentioned Shandorovka (15 kilometres west of Kvitki) was definitely in Soviet hands. It was not retaken in a counter-attack until 12 February. Group Stemmermann was not closed up around this location until ten days later, shortly before the breakout.

No documentary value can be placed therefore on Kalinov's account. For all that it is probable that Koniev said something similar at some time or other during that period. It shows how hopeless he considered the situation to be for XI Corps (Stemmermann) and XXXXII Corps (Lieb), and basically it was correct and accurate. Measured against what was humanly possible, Group Stemmermann was lost.

The hopes that had attended the capture of Kvitki on 2 February were not fulfilled. On 5 February Selimanov's Cossacks (V Soviet Guards

---

[4] *Sowjet-Marschälle haben das Wort*, pp.273, 274.

Cavalry Corps) stormed Olshana and then headed east past Kvitki towards Korsun. The danger of splintering our force was now gigantic. The outer perimeter still measured 250 kilometres. That was more than six weak divisions could defend against an offensive. In the north it was easy to draw the necessary conclusions. Loss of territory here was without significance. Three major breaches through XXXXII Corps accelerated the pulling back of the front to the line Staroselye–Yanovka in a large arc north around Korsun.

It was very much more difficult to give in to the idea of abandoning the arc around Vyasovok in the south. That would mean enlarging the distance to Eighth Army but Korsun lay – unfortunately – in the north and we depended for supply of provisions and ammunition from its airfield. By 8 February, 57th Infantry Division, the weak remnants of 389th Infantry Division and SS-Wiking struggled through to Gorodishche, forcing aside 72nd Infantry Division which on 9 February became the first unit to be freed. The gap east of Kvitki was closed by a counter-attack, and this marked the actual completion of our own pocket. There was now a cohesive front of about 130 kilometres perimeter around our central point of Korsun.

Our satisfaction at this improbable success, brought about by our own force and strength, was much subdued by news about the promised relief. XXXXVII Panzer Corps (von Vormann) lay firmly on the line Kapitanovka-Iskrennoye and tied down by a far superior enemy force. III Panzer Corps (Breith) was fighting west of Boyarka, 30 kilometres away. It had finally been given the order to regroup to attack eastwards to Komarovka but a deep penetration did not seem feasible even to the more senior ranks. As a precaution, on 6 February Eighth Army ordered preparations to be made for a breakout to the south-west as the last resort for its salvation.

What had been called forth by Hitler's great plans! Fifty thousand men fighting for their lives around Korsun, a weak panzer corps threatened at Boyarka with encirclement and a portentous giant gap in the outer front near Svenigorodka which we lacked the manpower to close. The bad news from the other armies, the fighting at Luga in the north, the loss of Apostolov and Nikopol nearer to us, hardly registered in comparison with our own concerns. All reaction tends to die away once a certain level is crossed.

The time to demand that the two encircled corps capitulate had been carefully chosen. The demand came from Marshal Zhukov. This best man of the Soviet generals always appeared when it became necessary to coordinate the operations of several army groups in decisive situations. When our radio monitoring came up with his name for the first time, major activity was always to be expected in the sector concerned.

On 8 February a Soviet General Staff colonel brought Zhukov's official ultimatum to us to lay down our weapons. The colonel duly appeared before our lines east of Medvin at 1430 hrs as parlementaire with bugler and white flag. The response was required by 1000 hrs on 9 February to be delivered by a plenipotentiary to Chirovka, a small village 15 kilometres west of Korsun, close to our front. Colonel Fouquet, leading officer of Corps Abteilung B, received the Russian colonel with correct observation of the traditional honours. The ultimatum was not answered, and the parlementaire was led back through our lines. The event was naturally reported to the highest level.

We were stupefied by the result. Hitler raged, demanding that Colonel Fouquet be court-martialled because he as a German officer had negotiated with the Soviets. It was in such moments that all his smouldering distrust of the Army flared up. He was too astute not to know the disapprobation which the old officer corps bore him and smelt treason everywhere since he himself did not understand the term loyalty. He did not understand that Germany and his own person were not identical in these crises.

There was no court-martial. Colonel Fouquet was protected by the Army: later this brave officer fell during the breakout.

To accompany this official action simultaneously, many thousand of leaflets containing a mixture of threats and promises were dropped over our lines. An example of this kind of psychological warfare is repeated verbatim here:

> To the Generals, Officers and Soldiers of the 11th and 42nd German Army Corps!
>
> Generals, officers and soldiers!
> The Red Army ring of encirclement around you is becoming more firm and narrow, your losses rise from day to day. All your lines of communication have

been cut. All attempts to send you help by transport aircraft will fail, for the Soviet Air Force is destroying your aircraft both in the air and on the ground. In two days alone – from 3 to 4 February – over one hundred Ju 52 transport aircraft were destroyed.

The attempts of the German 16th, 17th, 3rd, 13th, and 11th Panzer Divisions to break through the ring in order to release you have come to grief. These divisions were beaten, are themselves encircled and being wiped out by troops of the Red Army.

Your situation is hopeless and further resistance makes no sense. You would only be creating numerous victims uselessly.

Do not repeat the fatal error of those German soldiers and officers at Stalingrad who offered stubborn resistance in the hope of being relieved. They received no help. Field-Marshal von Manstein, the present commander-in-chief of Army Group South, tried to help the Stalingrad Army, but was beaten by the Red Army, and the German officers and soldiers who were hoping for Manstein's help and offered resistance are now dead.

After the conclusion of the battle of Stalingrad, the bodies of more than 147,200 dead German soldiers and officers were recovered and interred.

Now you yourselves can count on as little help as the German Army. Since the catastrophe at Stalingrad it has suffered defeat after defeat with colossal casualties and has become much weaker than it was last year.

The Red Army on the other hand has become much stronger. You know that you feel that to be true. Therefore, if you want to live, give yourself up!

An officer or soldier who gives himself up in this hopeless situation does not act dishonorably, but rationally. Military history has many examples in which the bravest soldiers and officers laid down their arms when further resistance was useless.

91,000 soldiers, 2,500 officers and 24 generals of the German Wehrmacht behaved rationally by giving themselves up led by Field Marshal von Paulus at Stalingrad.

Whoever surrenders is no longer our enemy. The Red Army Command guarantees to all soldiers, officers and generals who surrender, life and total security, medical treatment of the wounded and sick and a return home at the end of the war.

Form up in units and formations to surrender while it is not too late!

Whoever does not surrender will be put down mercilessly by our troops. You have the choice: life, or a senseless death.

On 7 February at 1140 hrs, Eighth Army ordered by radio (extract):

To liberate XI and XXXXII Corps the following will line up: XXXXVII Panzer Corps after regrouping with strong western flank from Yerki area passing

Kasazkoye to Olshana: III Panzer Corps from Vinograd area with right flank passing Lissyanka to Morenzy. Group Stemmermann will force breakthrough out of the encircling ring and advance with its strong concentration of forces on the inner flanks and under cover of flanks and rear towards the armoured spearheads across the line Shandorovka–Kvitki to Morenzy. Final timing of effect of armoured thrust groups dependent....

General Stemmermann, to whom XXXXII Corps (Lieb) had been subordinated at 0930 hrs on 7 February, set out purposefully to undertake the new assignment. With the whole pocket closed up – like a battleship – heading south-west, this meant going without any supply for an indefinite time. The Korsun airfield was the stake to which the group was tightly bound, although apart from only the most desperately urgent things, VIII Flieger Corps did not have the technical necessities for aerial drops. The airfield had to be held to the last moment despite that attempt to cooperate with III (Breith) and XXXXVII Panzer Corps (von Vormann).

This meant that first of all the situation and form of the pocket had to be changed. Instead of south-east to north-west – from Gorodishche to Yanovka – it had to stretch in length from Korsun as far to the south-west as possible. Following the logic of this, Kvitki, Gorodishche and Staroselye to the east, Yanovka to the north were evacuated and the foremost lines both sides of Korsun pulled back far enough that the airfield remained in service but not observable for enemy fire. This freed Corps Abteilung B and SS-Wiking one after the other: advancing to the south-west in company with 72nd Infantry Division they took Sharandovka on 10 February, Chilki and Komarovka on 12 February.

These difficult movements did not run smoothly. The Soviets fired concentrically from all sides into the narrow space of the pocket. The exhausted troops carried out the orders for the regrouping with much effort and dangerous delays. The technical communications set-up failed. Lack of ammunition, hunger, impassable tracks and severe weather caused crises of alarming proportions. The eastern front of the pocket in particular wavered. During the evacuation of Gorodishche the Soviets had made their appearance and torn open the line. Units intended for the advance of rescue to the south-west and pulling out for that purpose had to turn back to the east in order to prevent further breakthroughs.

The casualty lists increased to a disquieting level, on average three hundred men per day. Of particular concern were the approximately four thousand wounded who could not be transported out. In their signals, both corps called urgently for help and relief with a faster thrust especially of III Panzer Corps to Kkomarovka as our own forces were being fast diminished.

The welcome successes reported by III Panzer Corps (Breith) in its advance of 11 and 12 February allowed hope to revive. The decisive hour seemed to have come. Stemmermann gathered quite closely around Shandorovka the divisions entrusted to him. On the 13th Korsun was evacuated, on the 15th even Steblev to the south-west. Compressed into a space 7 by 8 kilometres in size, fifty thousand men waited for the order for them to align with the decisive final thrust by III Panzer Corps (Breith). They still hoped, but did not know yet that III Panzer Corps was spent, its advance bogged down in the mud.

Any attempt to pay fitting tribute to the achievements of commanders and men during the foregoing weeks would sound hollow. The superlatives are too clichéd. Before the curtain rises on the last act of the tragedy written by Hitler, it is to the enemy that we allow the final word. The frowning disapproval of a Graf Heinrich von Einsiedel may weigh heavier and be more valuable than any hymn of praise from this old soldier. Einsiedel's assertions show additionally the extent to which psychological warfare is of tantamount importance. In future wars it will place a burder on the front-line soldier, the scale of which we are not yet in a position to assess. Using any means, the other side will attempt to undermine confidence in the leadership and then even in the man at one's side in the field. If the soldier can be made to doubt the aims for which he is risking his life, he will stop fighting. No effort will be spared in order to attain that objective, no price will be too high to pay, for it will spare one's own blood.

Heinrich Graf von Einsiedel, Luftwaffe lieutenant, a Soviet prisoner-of-war since August 1942, then 22 years old and a leading member of the executive board of the National Committee *Freies Deutschland*, wrote:

> The Cherkassy Pocket has proved once again that there is no other solution than the immediate capitulation of the encircled units. On 3 February, the Red Army

succeeded in encircling nine infantry divisions, an SS–panzer division and an SS–brigade between Cherkassy and Byelaya Zerkov. Just like the Stalingrad Pocket, this pocket was handed by Hitler to the Soviets on a platter because under no circumstances was he prepared to evacuate this almost 100 kilometres long and only 20–30 kilometres wide projection of the front ...

Now Hitler has delivered his masterpiece. An almost 700-kilometre-long northern front has been created from the eastern front in the Ukraine. The laughably weak German forces are now more extended and weakened than ever. The Red Army had time for weeks to arrange its forces to cut off the narrow exit from the front-balcony on the Dnieper. This also offers us an unrepeatable opportunity for a decisive victory. If the commanders in the pocket decide to capitulate and ally with the Committee with a protest against Hitler, then it wil no longer be possible to simply pass us over in Germany – it would be a decisive beginning to the rebellion of the Wehrmacht against the system. Then the position of the Committee as regards the Soviets would be immeasurably stronger, then we would automatically gain weight which we could use for the benefit of prisoners of war.

How greatly the Soviet Government is interested in this opportunity is proved by the visit of Colonel-General Sharbakov, successor to Manuilski as Head of the Political Main Administration of the Red Army, to Seydlitz. Sharbakov is a Member of the Council of the Five, of the actual Soviet War Cabinet in which probably Stalin figures only as *Primus inter pares*.

Seydlitz, Korfes, Hadermann and Major Lewerenz went in the saloon coach of Shabakov's special train to the front to Army Group Watutin where Colonel Steidle and Major Büchler are already at work preparing a large-scale propaganda campaign against the pocket. All generals and senior officers in the National Committee have sent letters to the commanding officers known to them in the pocket, imploring them not to allow the pocket to become a second Stalingrad, to refuse Hitler obedience, by means of an orderly surrender to save immediately the lives of the 75,000 German soldiers entrusted to them and at the same time strike a decisive political blow against Hitler. Seydlitz and Korfes have addressed the encircled Staffs by radio and received confirmation of receipt. Germans and Russians wait to see if the commanding officers in the pocket will decide to accept an offer of negotiation with the Committee, but no answer has been received. ...

For the Soviets the battle is a new, great military victory, but for the Committee a decisive defeat ... the Generals have ignored us ...[5]

The data and figures argued by Graf Einsiedel are all false. Even Watutin (1st Ukrainian Front) is confused with Koniev (2nd Ukrainian Front).

---

[5] *Tagebuch der Versuchung*, Pontes Verlag 1950, pp.111–114.

To look for the reasons is futile. They are obvious. The only important thing in all of it is to know what worth the Russian leadership ascribed to the National Committee at that time and how it performed subsequently. The fact is that nothing was left untried to get our soldiers to refuse orders and mutiny. Loudspeakers droned day and night across the foremost front lines. Passes solemnly promising to every defector the best treatment fluttered down in their thousands from aircraft. All radio stations were called constantly and the climax was personal letters written to the senior commanders.

The individual leading members of the National Committee placed themselves as guarantors to their old acquaintances for the implementation of the far-reaching promises. Everything was assured, beginning with the best life in captivity to substantial influence in the reconstruction of the Reich, and all on one single condition: laying down of weapons. The pocket did not answer: the troops and their officers held to their oath.

With that the first major campaign of the National Committee *Freies Deutschland* came to grief and sealed its own fate. Stalin set aside the instrument to break up the German Wehrmacht which he himself had created. The only purpose of keeping up appearances was to sow discord amongst the prisoners of war and to have informers on the cheap in all camps.

After its unsuccessful debut the National Committee had no influence on military operations nor on the politics of the Kremlin. If one wishes, one can put this down to a success of the battle of Cherkassy.

On the German side the great danger which this propaganda concealed was recognised by all. In view of the unhappy situation on all fronts, in practice there was nothing that could be done about it but recognise it as an appeal to German soldiery. The orders passed down from above were in their naïveté and insincerity unsuitable for transmission to the troops and probably never got beyond the corps staffs.

Thus Hitler's order: 'The instigations transmitted "by Seydlitz" are to be seen as false propaganda. Arrest German prisoners of war sent back with letters from Russians!'

Precisely the many letters from Seydlitz to commanding officers he knew, dropped by Soviet aircraft attached to black-white-red banners, made reference to that kind of common personal experience such that there could be no doubt as to who sent them. To maintain that they were propaganda forgeries would never have been believed. Additionally Hitler himself changed his tune about these letters a few weks later when General von Seydlitz was sentenced to death in absentia for high treason and his close family arrested under the Sippenhaft law.

The second part of the quoted order was even less likely. No German soldier would have arrested a comrade who found himself back in his own lines after being in Soviet captivity.

Fortunately the Soviets themselves helped us. The fate and sufferings of German prisoners of war in Russia were too well known to tempt defectors. The enemy who wishes to lure men to desert must do more than just promise good treatment. If he then lets the defector starve to death, all the effort expended in propaganda is pointless. Precisely as pointless as calling upon a people to capitulate and offering nothing but terms of unconditional surrender and punishment. Such a proceeding only makes any sense when, certain of victory, the victor knowingly drives a beaten enemy into a desperate struggle which has his elimination as its purpose. As to deeds which create despair, these can be well argued from the Pharisee's chair.

CHAPTER 8

The breakout from the pocket

The breakout by Group Stemmermann, 16–17 February 1944 (Maps 10, 11)

The deadline came on 15 February. Relief by attacks of III Panzer Corps (Breith) or XXXXVII Panzer Corps (von Vormann) could no longer be expected.

At 1105 hrs Eighth Army ordered by radio:

> Ability to act of III Panzer Corps limited by weather and supply conditions. Group Stemmermann must make a decisive breakthrough to a point 2 kilometres south of Dzhurshenzy – Height 239.0 by own resources. There link up with III Panzer Corps. The breakthrough wedge is to force the breach led by Lieutenant-General Lieb, XXXXII Army Corps embracing all attacking forces especially SS-Wiking supported by the mass of the artillery. No partial attacks!

The *plan* for the breakout was already in place. At 2300 hrs on 16 February, the breakout group, in three deeply staggered attack spearheads, was to depart from the line Chilki–Komarovka, work foward silently without artillery preparation and assault the enemy with bayonets and 'Hurra!' at one go, forcing through to the Dzhurshenzy–Height 239.0 line and there link up with III Panzer Corps (Breith).

The three attack groups at the readiness points and in the battle area were:

Right: Corps Abteilung B Chilki direction of thrust over high ground south of Petrovskoye (234.1) – Dzhurshenzy South.
Centre: 72nd Infantry Division gully 1.5 kilometres south-east Chilki, direction of thrust northern edge woodland south-east Dzhurshenzy – north 239.0 – Oktyabr.
Left: 5.SS-Panzer Division *Wiking* Komarovka direction of thrust parallel to 72nd Infantry Division passing south of 239.0.

At daylight, VIII Flieger Corps would cover the flanks, III and XXXXVII Panzer Corps by a continuation of their attacks in the former direction draw upon themselves and tie down as many as possible of the enemy.

The divisions had to organise themselves into three sections: bayonet section (infantry assault force); heavy weapons; artillery and support/ rearward services.

The rearguard composed of 57th and 88th Infantry Divisions had to cover the backs of the breakthrough group from a flat arc around Shandorovka and set off upon receiving a codeword by radio; 57th Infantry Division on the breakthrough path of SS-Wiking; 88th Infantry Division on that of 72nd Infantry Division.

Artillery, panzers, assault guns and other heavy weapons were to be included and deployed dependent on their mobility and the ammunition situation, the remainder were to be destroyed.

For their own perhaps still possible salvation, orders were given for about 1,500 wounded to be left at Shandorovka with medical staff and the necessary care personnel. The later course of events justified this measure.

The carrying out of the preparations for the advance caused difficulties and friction of uncommon proportions on 15 and 16 February. The only route for three divisions, all the support and all the rearward services of the two corps led through Shandorovka. Movement through the deep mud was agonisingly slow. Because they could not escape from the view of the enemy, the masses were exposed to continuous aimed fire of artillery, Stalin's organs [Katyusha rocket launchers] and heavy mortars.

Wrecked vehicles, burning ammunition waggons, the remains of walls, flaming wooden houses blocked the single narrow road. Smoke and fumes, cries, the whimpering of the severely wounded and the barking of our flak guns filled the air, interspersed with the howling of our artillery fire. The guns which had to be destroyed fired their last rounds. Low-level bombing and strafing from the air completed the hell in the village. Despite everything, new units continued to flow in from north, east and south. There was no way to go round it, and only in the west did freedom beckon.

'Freedom' was also the official password of the day.

All telephone lines had been long since torn up. Radio equipment mounted on horse-drawn waggons was only partially serviceable and irregular. To the extent that reports from the front reached General Stemmermann at Chilki, they showed the enemy effort to crush the alarmingly shrinking pocket by concentric attacks.

South of Steblev in the north-east, Soviet tanks attacked the rearguard divisions (57th and 88th Infantry Divisions) as they moved out but the latter succeeded eventually in sealing off the dangerous breach. Closer than intended – up to three kilometres – the foremost line had advanced to Shandarovka where the wedged-in masses had assembled. All leadership influence here was threatening to fade away.

In the south-west the seething fighting around Komorovka against SS-Wiking flared up on the 16th. Apparently the Soviets could not get over the loss of the village. During the morning it changed hands four times. Here too the foremost front line was pressing within three kilometres of Shandarovka. The readiness positions planned for the area were no longer viable. With heavy heart we discarded the idea of an immediate counter-attack but we could not risk creating another trouble spot prematurely, the danger of attracting fresh enemy forces to the area was too great and could flaw our moment of surprise at 2300 hrs. It seemed better, despite all objections, to move the assembly area back. The order had to be passed to the units but it did not get through to them all. 'Order, counter-order, disorder'. Napoleon was right again.

The pocket was under great pressure and all the valves were shut. Every tear in the protecting ring was bound to lead to an explosion which here would mean panic and chaos. Fifty thousand men within 50 square kilometres with all their equipment. That kind of compressed mass is no longer manouevrable and removed from all leadership. Only when the ordered hour struck would it set off in the direction ordered. Only then would there be hope of freedom.

The hours passed with agonising tension, much too slowly for excited nerves and much too quickly – so it seemed – for carrying out the ordered regrouping. It went on and on with no end in sight.

Every troop officer knew the time span during which he was not to intrude, for every intrusion by him could only bring confusion to the precisely measured course of the movements, to the orders of his NCOs which he would not know. These hours of inactivity, in which heart and mind asked constantly: Have you done everything humanly possible, can you answer for what is happening here? would cause anguish under normal circumstances, here at Chilki the responsibility was gigantic, for there was no longer any alternative. There was only: breakout as ordered. At any price! All bridges to the past were down.

Together with all surplus weapons and equipment, all papers, files and baggage were burnt. Separation from dear everyday things, souvenirs, to which the heart clung, all one's possessions, was a heavy blow. All that remained was what one needed in close combat and could carry.

Darkness came with frost and snow flurries. The worse the weather the greater the probability that our surprise would succeed. The enemy still seemed to have noticed nothing. His firing became weaker and less regular. Even in Shandorovka the situation was becoming disentangled, and one after another the attack groups reported the end of the alert. The decisive hour approached.

At 2300 hrs the first section of the three attack groups appeared without softening-up fire. The totally surprised enemy was overrun, his response slight. The ring was opened and so far as could be ascertained the breakout must succeed – if III Panzer Corps (Breith) was still at Dzhurshenzy, on Hill 239 and at Potshapinzy. The last radio message at 1500 hrs stated: 'Oktyabr taken'.

With that the planned leadership of the Stemmermann Group and its existence ended.

Since the preconditions for the success of the desperate III Panzer Corps (Breith) operation could not be fulfilled, the further losses would involve a race of the individual with death in which all units had disintegrated. The influence of the officer reached only so far as his voice carried. The elementary pull of the following masses was impossible to control.

The course of events over the following hours is therefore difficult to piece together. The only sources are the confused and contradictory individual reports of the survivors. There were no longer troop staff or command officers.

The arrival of the second and third sections from the waiting areas went ahead according to plan under the spell of the successful breakout of the first section. Around forty thousand men flowed to the west in a constantly growing stream. Only a few kilometres had to be covered and then one would meet up with comrades hurrying to the relief!

Terrible was the disappointment and horror when at daybreak approaching Dzhurshenzy-Potchapinzy, the densely grouped mass was met by murderous tank, anti-tank and artillery fire. Until now the troops had carried all their heavy equipment through the deep, snow-encrusted gullies. All was now smashed to pieces by the enemy shelling. Guns and assault guns came to a standstill after their ammunition was expended. Here the wounded brought along by the troops met their fate.

Now the masses arose, left completely to their own devices and with nothing but the weapons they held in their own hands, and with the courage born of despair began searching for a way out of the chaos. Formations of hundreds of soldiers, tossed together from all branches of service and units, were led by the remaining officers onwards towards the West. Enemy infantry were brushed aside with knife, entrenching tool and bayonet, even their tanks turned away. But the Soviets continued to pour their fire into the unprotected, routed mass as it surged blindly onwards. The losses rose.

The Soviets had set up defences along the Dzhurshenzy-Potchapinzy line while the divisions of III Panzer Corps (Breith) were fighting around Chishinzy, Oktyabr and at Lissyanka for the crossing over the Gniloi Tikich.

Only individual small groups succeeded in breaking through under cover of darkness and snowfall. At Oktyabr they ran into German panzers and were saved. The mass was forced to ground and lay there initially without hope.

At daybreak, in desperation individuals headed to the south where the sound of fighting seemed less. By herd instinct the mass followed.

Seeing their crazed approach, Soviet infantry fled from the eastern part of Potchapinzy leaving the way free. At the banks of the Gniloi Tikich the enemy river defence was blown from the rear. There was no bridge, however, and the ice covering the river had broken. Under pressure from tanks, artillery and constantly increasing infantry, the swarm, crammed together and abandoning their last hand weapons, threw themselves into the icy river where many drowned. Those that reached the other side, frozen to the marrow and wet through, were not necessarily saved, for from the long, open ridge south-east of Lissyanka, the fire of T-34s and artillery could pursue them. Whoever was not hit, or did not freeze to death, was eventually rescued in the southern part of Lissyanka by 1st Panzer Division.

Many hundreds lost their lives here at Gniloi Tilich, in sight of the goal of which they had dreamed these last weeks.

Some of the last men of the rearguard, who in exemplary fulfillment of duty had remained engaged with the enemy, managed to regain the German lines during the night of 17 February. Half frozen and starving, without weapons, the latest events beyond their comprehension, in the intended interception area north of Uman they joined twenty to twenty-five thousand other German soldiers. Their endless questions as to the sense of the entire operation remained unanswered. Whoever had survived the hell of this 21-day-long battle was no longer fit for the front physically. The damage to the morale of the troops was irreparable. They had lost their confidence in the leadership.

XI Corps (Stemmermann) and XXXXII Corps (Lieb) had ceased to exist. Their removal from the front created the pre-conditions for the great Soviet breakthrough in March across the Bug and Dniester as far as Pruth.

CHAPTER 9

Victory celebrations on both sides

Victory Celebrations on both sides after 17 February 1944

In the battle of Cherkassy an unusually high degree of accomplishment by the troops of both sides was matched by an unusual accumulation of errors at the highest level of leadership. On the German side, a rational leadership would never have accepted battle for the projecting bend in the front under the given circumstances. On the Soviet side, the operational possibilities which were brought about by tactical success, were not exploited. The successful thrust to the Pruth in March would, if taken in January, have meant for Army Group von Manstein a devastating battle to avoid encirclement in the Ukraine and Bessarabia with a reversed front and with no possibility of supply. A bolder approach might have brought an end to the war at the beginning of 1944. Instead the Soviets contented themselves with 'common or garden' victories, attacked at Nikopol–Krivoi Rog frontally and despite a much greater numerical superiority did not prevent the breakout even here. Accordingly both sides had an interest in drowning all criticism by grandiloquent announcements.

For the Soviets it was easier. Their tactical victory could not be doubted. On 20 February Stalin celebrated the Battle of Kanev–Korsun with a Special Order of the Day. He reported: Ten German divisions with a total strength of ninety thousand men wiped out, fifty-five thousand found dead on the battlefield, 18,200 prisoners.

Koniev, commander-in-chief of 2nd Ukrainian Front was promoted with due solemnity to Marshal of the Red Army; Rotmistrov, commander-in-chief of 5th Guards Tank Army was appointed Marshal of the Tank Arm.

On the German side the official bulletins of the High Command of the Wehrmacht (OKW) were at first sober and factual:

From Führer Headquarters, 18 February.

After fighting off powerful counter-attacks in the area west of Cherkassy, contact was restored with a strong German battle group cut off for weeks after it fought through to the front to meet the panzer units sent to its relief.

From Führer Headquarters, 19 February.

West of Cherkassy further elements of the freed battle group were reintegrated after fighting off numerous enemy counter-attacks and despite the most difficult conditions of terrain.

Then it became bombastic.

From Führer Headquarters, 20 February.

Furthermore the High Command of the Wehrmacht (OKW) makes known in addition to the reported relief of the encircled German battle group west of Cherkassy:

The reintegration of the freed divisions had been completed. The Army and Waffen-SS troops led by General of Artillery Stemmermann and Lieutenant-General Lieb cut off since the 28 January held off the attack by a far superior enemy force in an heroic defensive battle and then in bitter fighting broke through the enemy's encirclement. In so doing, officers and men have added a further shining example of heroic endurance, brave fighting spirit and willing sacrifice to the annals of German military history.

The Army and Waffen-SS units commanded by General of Panzer Troops Breith in cooperation with the troops led by Lieutenant-General von Vormann which went to the relief of the battle group in the most difficult conditions of weather and terrain met the preconditions for the breakthrough by the exemplary contribution of every single soldier.

The Soviets suffered the heaviest casualties and between 4 and 18 February lost 728 tanks and assault guns: 800 guns were captured and several thousand prisoners taken.

VIII Flieger Corps under Lieutenant-General Seidemann provided exemplary support to the heavily engaged Army troops in proven brotherhood in arms. Transport and ground attack units supplied the encircled forces in difficult weather conditions and in the face of strong enemy fighter and anti-aircraft defences, supplying them with ammunition, provisions and fuel and bringing out over 2,400 wounded. During this operation 32 transport aircraft were lost, 58 enemy aircraft were shot down in aerial combat and by flak.

In the following days too the columns of an obedient press were filled with the usual individual reports of the Propaganda Ministry about the battles, men being received by the Führer, promotions, the award of decorations and the like.

Skilful propaganda misted over and and reworked the fact that a great battle had been lost with serious casualties. The troops involved read with astonishment and incredulity that they had fought and won a great victory – at Cherkassy 1944 in the Ukraine.

Appendix

German troop formations involved in the fighting, 5 January–17 February 1944

Eighth Army

XI Army Corps
XXXXII Army Corps
LII Army Corps
XXXXVII Panzer Corps
57th Infantry Division
72nd Infantry Division
88th Infantry Division
106th Infantry Division
282nd Infantry Division
320th Infantry Division
376th Infantry Division
384th Infantry Division
Corps Abteilung A,
    Corps Abteilung B
Group Haack (Leave-taker unit)
10th Panzer-Grenadier Division
Panzer-Grenadier Division
    Grossdeutschland
3rd Panzer Division
11th Panzer Division
13th Panzer Division
14th Panzer Division
24th Panzer Division
2nd Parachute (Fallschirmjäger) Division
3rd SS-Panzer Division Totenkopf
5th SS-Panzer Division Wiking
SS-Volunteer (Freiwilligen) Brigade
    Wallonien

First Panzer Army

VII Army Corps
III Panzer Corps
34th Infantry Division
198th Infantry Division
1st Panzer Division
16th Panzer Division
17th Panzer Division
Leibstandarte SS Adolf Hitler
VIII Flieger Corps

Index